RIDING
THE
MINOTAUR

RIDING
THE
MINOTAUR

by

Scott Davies

EFSTATHIADIS GROUP

EFSTATHIADIS GROUP S.A.
14, Valtetsiou Str.
106 80 Athens
Tel: (01) 5154650, 6450113
Fax: (01) 5154657
GREECE

ISBN 960 226 581 7

© **Efstathiadis Group S.A. 1999**

All rights reserved; no part of this
publication may be reproduced, stored in a
retrieval system or transmitted, in any form
or by any means, electronic, mechanical,
photocopying, recording, or otherwise, without the
prior permission of Efstathiadis Group S.A.

Printed and bound in Greece

CONTENTS

INTRODUCTORY NOTES 7

CHAPTER ONE. HOW NOT TO BUY A HOUSE 9

CHAPTER TWO. A TOILET IN THE COURTYARD 23

CHAPTER THREE. BATTLE WITH BUREAUCRACY 37

CHAPTER FOUR. CONSTRUCTING A DREAM FROM A WRECK 55

CHAPTER FIVE. CAFENIA, CAMARADERIE AND KLEPTOCRATS 69

CHAPTER SIX. AN EVENING WITH HOMER 95

CHAPTER SEVEN. RATS AND WINTER FUEL 113

CHAPTER EIGHT. CELEBRATIONS CRETAN STYLE 133

CHAPTER NINE. TOIL FOR OIL 145

CHAPTER TEN. THE RURAL LIFE 167

CHAPTER ELEVEN. HOME COOKING 187

CHAPTER TWELVE. INCENSE AND THE EVIL EYE 199

CHAPTER THIRTEEN. RIDING THE MINOTAUR 223

CHAPTER FOURTEEN. EXPLORING CRETE 239

CHAPTER FIFTEEN. SETTLING IN 263

APPENDIX ONE. SEASONS 281

APPENDIX TWO. SELECTED BIBLIOGRAPHY 291

INTRODUCTORY NOTES

Scott Davies is really two people, Paula Scott, an oceanographer, and Mike Davies, a metallurgist. Together we operate our own small, independent consulting company, mostly solving corrosion problems in marine environments. We were able to move to Crete because our work is international, so location of our home and office was immaterial as long as we have a phone and fax. This freedom of choice meant that, as long as our customers could still find us, we could live in Crete and travel from there wherever and whenever we were needed.

Because of the multiple use of common first names in the village, such as Manolis, Maria, etc., we have adopted the Welsh practice of appending occupation or other distinguishing features to clarify which individual we are referring to. For example, the Welsh Evans the Milk or Dai the Bread becomes Manolis the Taverna or Michalis the Cafenion.

Where we have included Greek words in the text we have used spellings that we hope will facilitate pronunciation by non-Greek-speakers. The selection of words in Greek to include in the text has been made largely on the basis of very common usage, Cretan dialect or to explain some confusion or other that has be-devilled us.

Our research for this book has included many interrogative conversations with people in the village and elsewhere. We have also relied heavily on extensive background reading from many sources. A select bibliography of the published sources that we have found most helpful is Appendix Two.

CHAPTER ONE

How Not to Buy a House

We bought our house from a notice in a public toilet.

We weren't really looking for one and we had no money. Three days later we had bought a stone ruin and resolved to move to Crete, seduced by the magic of the island and the wily charm of a master salesman.

Our only previous contact with Greece had been a holiday with friends in Corfu the preceding year. We fell in love with the climate, the Greek people and their approach to life. Like almost every tourist we began an idle fantasy about living on a Mediterranean island, so when we were confronted with the toilet notice we thought there would be no harm in asking.

The small typed sign was in the gents in a curry restaurant in Hersonissos. After the fourth beer, Mike came back with it and read,

> "LOOKING FOR PROPERTY IN CRETE?
> WE HAVE FARMHOUSES, VILLAGE HOUSES
> & BUILDING PLOTS."

This was followed by a phone number.

"You are not going to call a number you found on the wall of a public toilet", said our incredulous friends. "There isn't even an agent or company name."

The next day Paula called the number.

"You have properties for sale?"

"Yes, how did you get our number?" was the reply in impeccable English.

"Uh, I'll tell you later, where are you?"

"Heraklion."

"We're in Hersonissos, we'll be there in an hour or so."

The office was tucked away in a tortuous alley within the old walled city and had no sign hanging outside or any other indications of permanency. In fact, the only clue that we had found the right place was our telephone friend hanging out of the second floor window beckoning us.

Lawrence Mefsut, a cosmopolitan and much-travelled Cretan, is 60ish, red-faced, short and fat with cigarette stains on his fingers and white rings around his irises, giving incontrovertible evidence that he is a living exception to the rule about smoking, cholesterol and survival prospects. But, bless his battered body, he actually had photographs of some derelict houses, which is all he said we could afford in our price range. One was a wall, a very old picturesque stone wall but only one wall, standing in isolation in a field. We agreed it would be criminal to destroy it and yes, a very nice house could be built around it.

Yes, but...

He was, he claimed not an agent at all, but an estate broker. His business consisted of buying houses, or the option on them, from locals in the villages. Advertising through agents abroad, he tried to resell them at vast profit to English and

German romantics looking for an annual two weeks of the "simple life". He was willing to show us some places today, "now, come with me!" We went.

Lawrence drives like he lives and confirms our theory that he is terrified of nothing except old age. Mike is cleverer than Paula and refused to sit in the front seat. After a detour to collect his "scout" (he has a scout in several villages, looking for potential houses), we drove into the hills. Lawrence spent the drive telling us the story of his life. He has lived all over Europe, where he picked up fluent English and German. He has had two wives, and some children, not necessarily by the wives. He clearly loved people and selling, although he didn't seem to have been in this (or any other) job very long. He was an amiable salesman, with a skill in storytelling which would have been revered by the ancients. We liked him because he reminded us of Paula's father. Somewhat naively, for the same reason we trusted him too.

A house in the hills was our choice, we did not desire and could not afford a place on the coast. On arrival at a village, much like the rest, we were bundled out of the car and placed at a cafenion (cafe) table. The scout, Yannis, disappeared, while Lawrence leisurely ordered coffee and watermelon. After a civilized interval we strolled up the hill (there is always a hill but this one was steeper than usual).

"This is your house."

We looked around, and didn't actually see a house, only a narrow street with a long wall, occupying most of the block. Meantime, Yannis was opening a gate and Lawrence waved us in with a grand flourish. Inside were three buildings surrounded by a courtyard with several overgrown fruit trees, outdoor oven and disused well.

And a toilet. Right out in the open in the courtyard, a ceramic throne, minus seat, minus cistern, but with a matching cover.

Inside the buildings were four terracotta olive jars and a feature we soon came to expect in all old Cretan houses, the wine press, a vast stone tub 2 m sq into which grapes are tossed for crushing by the old-fashioned method of stomping. A small spout at the bottom leads to a depression in the floor where the juice is collected. Lawrence suggested we make it a "feature" by perching a large bed on top of it.

Standing among grape vines growing over onto the second floor balcony we admired the panoramic view of other village houses and the vineyards, olive groves and hillsides beyond. Approximately how many months per year did we plan to spend here, Lawrence asked.

"Approximately twelve." He raised his eyebrows.

We saw a hillside plot and two more houses in the same village, both in similar states of repair, but with less potential for our rampant imaginations. Lawrence then insisted on taking us for lunch and after several more barely believable tales promised to show us one more house in another, higher village south of Rethymnon the next day. We were to meet him at his office at 10 am sharp because he had several other engagements in different villages. We arrived at 10:01 and all departed for the next door cafenion for coffee and, in Lawrence's case, breakfast.

We arrived at the property about noon. Walking into the back room we startled the inhabitant, who snorted and oinked angrily at us. The house was in better repair than the others we had seen, and apart from needing a cesspit or septic tank, was immediately habitable. Nonetheless, we rejected this house largely on the grounds that someone mentioned there is snow in the village in winter. We weren't going to move all the way to the most southerly point in Europe only to be snowed on!

We were dropped off by Lawrence near the Rethymnon bus stop, at one of the tavernas which spring up along the main road of all the tourist routes, and asked the time of the next bus. In about one or two hours we were told. Perfect. We ordered our first retsina of the day just as we saw the Rethymnon bus rounding the corner. A forty yard dash precluded any speculation about local knowledge. Half an hour later we finally retired to a taverna in Rethymnon, thoroughly exhausted by Lawrence's energy and stories, for a serious discussion of our purchasing prospects.

The crux of the discussion went something like this: Crete was clearly the place of our dreams. None of the houses we had been shown were ideal. For one thing, none of them fulfilled our first prerequisite of a substantial garden. If we rejected them all, we could ask Lawrence to locate something nearer our requirements. Then we would come back here again, look, reject and spend the next twenty years thinking and talking about our dream. Or we could just go ahead and buy a house from Lawrence and get on with living in it.

"Well, what do you want to do?"

"What the hell, let's do it."

Thus, after the long, logical, rational reflection required by a substantial uprooting and the purchase of a new house, the decision was made.

After very few glasses of wine, another decision was clear, we wanted the first house we had seen. There was only one minor snag - we had no money with us. Even in our wildest dreams we had not expected to buy a house on this holiday. More seriously, since the house was more than we had expected, we weren't sure we had sufficient money at all. We did some rough calculations, based on the premise that you should always go for the luxuries in life, the basics will take care of themselves. We knew that there were several invoices outstanding from clients who were overdue with payment. In the end we decided, on no information and with less logic, that there would be no problem. After all, didn't Lawrence offer an interest free loan for 20% of the amount? How could we lose?

We turned to the more pleasant prospect of planning our new house and were shortly embroiled in a discussion of the exact location of the fireplace. We made bets and each drew out from memory our own plan of the house. We also plotted how to get Lawrence to take us back to it for a second visit after we had agreed to buy. Since we had already taken up two days of his exhausting schedule we thought it would take some manoeuvring on our part to achieve a visit which would settle the bet.

The last day of our holiday was a Saturday, but Lawrence nevertheless agreed to meet us in his office to hear our decision. We anticipated some hard bargaining, because we wouldn't buy the house without the olive jars and we wanted him to find a phone line from someone in the village. Waiting for a phone in Crete through normal channels can take upwards of 5 years but for a few hundred pounds Lawrence said he should be able to persuade someone to sell the transfer of their line. A phone/fax line was essential if we were to run our consulting business here.

We entered the negotiations with the good news, bad news tactic.

"First, the good news. We want the first house."

"Then what could be the bad news?"

"We want the olive jars, too."

"Done. Next?"

"We want a phone."

"I can't make it a written condition of sale, but I'll give you my word."

"Good enough."

As easy as that. We had been out-negotiated by a pro.

The next thing was to break the news that we didn't have any money with us. We suggested we send it to him from Canada, and then he could send us the deed in exchange.

"I'm glad you suggested that, not me", was the laconic reply.

In fact, there was a more acceptable, legal mechanism. We would go to a solicitor and give her the power of attorney to buy the house. We would send her the money and she would collect the deed and check that it was clear. No problem, Lawrence knew just the person, whom we could visit immediately.

A few phone calls were required to set it up. A snag developed because the solicitor said we, being residents of Canada, couldn't own property in Greece. Lawrence began to argue that our EU passports were relevant, not our residence. Since January, 1991 any resident of a European Union country has the legal right to live and work in any other EU country. He turned red, twitched, shouted. We glanced at each other, each regretting that we had not taken a Cardio-Pulmonary Resuscitation course, knowing we had a type A heart attack in progress. Suddenly, Lawrence hung up the phone and smiled at us; no problem, the law is clear and we do have EU passports. Ergo, we may buy a Greek house. We strolled down the street to the notary and solicitor, both of whom were necessary for this transaction. Both were apparently friends of Lawrence, neither spoke a word of English.

Paula created a furore and nearly precipitated another heart attack when she refused to conform to the standard Greek practice of defining women as property of their fathers and husbands. By one of those accidents of life she is known professionally and legally by the name of her divorced husband. Consequently, she declined to be identified by her maiden name, as is common practise in Greece, believing that if she were to be a property owner the name on the deed should coincide with other identification documents she possessed. Then she refused to play again; she would not be defined as the property of her first husband, whose names and particulars were then requested. She contended with some logic that a long divorced husband on another continent could not possibly be relevant to the matter in hand. Who on earth did she belong to? She and Mike were not married in Greek law, so she couldn't belong to him either. Though visibly upset at being unable to ascribe ownership in the confusion of names and relationships, they finally agreed to proceed with the available information. What else could they do, torture it out of her? After all, they already had our names, dates and places of birth and the names, birth date and birth place of both our fathers and mothers. We reckoned that should be sufficient for identification purposes.

The notary drew up the document in Greek for the solicitor, for which an official translation was required by Greek law. Lawrence acted as official translator. The completed document was smothered by the notary with 10 official, colourful, government stamps and pounded in triplicate with several satisfyingly loud rubber stamps in the Chinese manner, chop chop. The gist of it was that when we paid the lawyer the money Lawrence would hand her the deed.

Finally it was all over. We had just committed ourselves to send the average annual wage to a stranger to whom we were introduced by a public toilet, on the strength of a document we couldn't read, in the hope of buying a house we had only seen once, briefly and which we knew was derelict. We couldn't even remember where the fireplace was. Worse than that, we wouldn't have been able to find the house again on our own.

Lawrence shook our hands in congratulations, or perhaps in amazement at our naivety and said we must see the house again after lunch. We were astonished and grateful that he would spend still more time allowing us a second visit now that we had bought the place.

"Our relationship only begins when you buy the house," he said "you must trust me or we can not do business together."

He also suggested coyly that it was traditional for the buyer to pay for lunch. We readily agreed, who were we to buck tradition? Lawrence had been hosting us magnificently for two days. He knew just the place, follow him. We did and he did. It was down by the port, with excellent food and very inexpensive. We have since become regular patrons there.

We drove once more to the village, which now had a name for us, Kato Asites. We stopped at the same cafenion while Lawrence tried unsuccessfully to locate the keys from the old lady who owned the house. When they weren't to be found he borrowed a ladder from the neighbour to scale the wall and let us at least look at the outside of the buildings. While Lawrence was loudly and confidently volunteering to have a team repair the roof before the rains to prevent further damp problems, we examined the tiles closely. It was clear to us that the roof had already been repaired recently and was just about the only part of the house which WASN'T in need of urgent repair. The damp was coming from the balcony, where water was trapped by the vines and ran down the walls. We declined assistance and said we'd be back before the rains for a closer look.

We also settled our bet. The fireplace was neither on the north nor the west wall, but in one of the other buildings, the old kitchen, which was separate from the main house. It reminded us of some advice that a sensible friend had given us about making precise notes on every property we visited. We remembered that advice again several weeks later when we realized we didn't have the address of our house.

We returned home in triumph to discover that the unpaid invoices were still unpaid and even if they had been, we'd over-estimated our cash in hand by about 20% of the purchase price. Mike had to leave again immediately on business, while Paula tried to negotiate a short term loan quickly. Lawrence's parting advice was to hurry the money across because the old lady was on her last legs and we didn't want to start negotiations again with all her heirs, did we? No, we did not, we would send the money immediately on our return. It took nearly a month, during which time the old lady apparently enjoyed excellent health.

We dined out for the next three weeks on the story of what all our friends called our Very Expensive Holiday In Crete. We waited, sublimely confident. And waited, tentatively confident. And waited, clinging to hope that a postal strike in Canada had been the cause of delay, grateful that we had not yet sent the balance, at least. Finally we received evidence that Lawrence's company had not disappeared. He acknowledged receipt of the first payment and the transfer document should arrive soon. We waited still longer, then faxed him the message that we would be in Crete at the end of October to visit the house again. He would have the documents waiting, he faxed back. He had booked our hotel, "have a good trip and wish you well". By the way, he had not yet received the balance of the funds.

Well, he didn't have to tell us that, we knew we were going to take the bank draft with us to make sure the house, complete with olive jars, was in order before paying the balance. We were, after all, sensible businessmen!

Oddly enough, we went back in late October and the hotel had been booked, the house, complete with jars, was in order and Lawrence gave us the transfer papers and the keys. The front door key, which we took home with us as proof of our success, measures a magnificent 15 cm in length and weighs almost 100 g. We dined out several more times with our friends on the strength of that medieval key.

So, even before we had the transfer document translated, we knew that, in spite of all our witlessness, our faith had been rewarded and we had actually purchased a house in Crete - #260 Agia Paraskevi, Kato Asites. We hoped to have our first visitors as soon as we had put a curtain around the toilet.

Oh, and by the way, we subsequently heard that Lawrence intended to take out a franchise on all the restaurant toilets in Crete.

As Lawrence would say, we wish him well.

CHAPTER TWO

A TOILET IN THE COURTYARD

It was only after we had spent much more time in Crete that we realized the magnitude of our achievement in buying a village house in three days. We learned later that it is very difficult to purchase property anywhere in Greece because there is no developed property market. You never see those handy little shops with pictures of houses in the windows and neatly printed prices underneath. There is hardly a need for real estate agents since until Greece merged with the European market in 1991 it was illegal for foreigners to purchase property in many parts of Greece.

Had we been aware of the difficulties, we would have been completely daunted by the prospect of buying in a foreign language and culture. Every property has potentially dozens of owners. Greek inheritance laws state that, in the absence of a will (and sometimes even despite one) property is divided between the spouse and children, if any. In the absence of these, a complicated formula apportions the property to a variety of relatives, in order of their relatedness. Many of the co-owners, we were warned too late, could be living abroad. Thus, we might well have unwittingly paid full price for a small fraction of a house. Buying property is further complicated by the fact that most people have no papers to prove their ownership and official surveys indicating precise boundaries often do not exist. It is simply known and accepted that property is inherited from parents and is passed down through the generations.

Furthermore, we learned that the reason we had not found

the isolated farmhouse of our dreams is because Cretans live in villages and travel daily to their numerous scattered fields. This is why villages are all one comfortable donkey day distant.

As we came to know more about our neighbours and life in Crete, we were grateful that we did choose to live in the centre of a thriving village. Our lives here have been tremendously enriched by proximity to friends, shops, celebrations and simple opportunities to chat and gossip. We compare our life with that of another foreigner who bought a holiday house in an abandoned village. She can not nip out for a loaf of bread. She never knows any of the interesting gossip and latest happenings. She knows very few people and the only neighbour who comes to visit her is a local woman who has a summer home nearby for temporary residence during the growing season.

All this we learned much later. We had bypassed all these difficulties in sublime ignorance. By tremendous good luck we had bought our house from a childless widow. In the meantime, our first trip to Crete after buying the house was made with the objective of assessing the repair work needed prior to our move. On our arrival in Heraklion we realized with embarrassment that we still could not without assistance find our own house! Luckily, we were driven to the village and escorted to the property by one of Lawrence's associates, frantically memorizing the route from the village square. After a few polite exchanges we were left alone with our purchase.

Probably all amateur house buyers never truly see with honest eyes the prospective properties they view. Certainly we didn't. While the clever Lawrence extolled the virtues of any meagrely attractive features our naive mind's eyes were imagining ourselves sipping sundowners on the balcony with our view of the lower village and distant vineyards and olive groves. The enormous downstairs room was transformed into a cosy, old-fashioned kitchen/living room with the olive jars scattered casually to lend authenticity to the ancient Greek ambience.

Now, however, the place was ours. Here was our moment of truth. As we wandered uncertainly across the overgrown courtyard every crack in the stonework leapt out to glare at us. Gaps between the flat roof and stone walls on the ground floor were large enough to permit entry of the Trojan horse. Wind whistled through great breaches in the front door where the wood had rotted and where previous owners had changed their mind about the correct location of the keyhole.

With dampened spirits we inserted the great key into the lock and commenced our tour. The front room had dripped moisture from the green walls with long rivulets tracing a merry path from the electricity box. Solid drops of dirt hung from the end of the one naked bulb hanging in the middle of the room. We dared not try the light switches, for fear of what we might see clearly as much as for electrical safety.

Mike bumped his head on the inner door as we passed into the dimly lit back room. A windowless gap high up near the ceiling provided the only natural light, curtailed by the staircase cutting across it to the upper floor. An old gas burner rested casually on an irregular dirt floor against a rough stone wall. Two broken chairs tilted drunkenly in the gloom, framing a dead rat. We stumbled over scattered paving stones artfully decorated with sheep droppings and squeezed through a tiny door to the staircase. Here concrete had been poured to form a water trough for the livestock. It drained into a plastic pipe which traversed the kitchen and disappeared mysteriously into the outer wall next to the courtyard. When in use the trough must have acted as a footbath for anyone descending from upstairs. The water in the trough had rotted out the supports leaving the stairs freely suspended in space.

We climbed the stairs gingerly, one at a time. We passed a blocked up south-facing window and surveyed the one-roomed upper floor. A grimy east window let light in, mostly from the decaying window frame and collapsing lintel. For extra light we lowered the heavy iron security bars and opened the balcony doors. Light flooded onto the grey floorboards and made dancing dust particles from the ankle deep supply we had disturbed. The doors were framed with bright green cracks and more rivulets. Ignoring this and anticipating our magnificent view we rushed outside, Mike's head again grazing the sagging lintel.

Stepping out onto the debris and rocks fallen from the upper storey wall we picked our way to the unprotected edge of the verandah. So much for our sundowners, the view faced east, toward the morning sun. Furthermore, from this view we could clearly see that our neighbours across the narrow lane were close to completion of an upper floor room for their adult son. From his new balcony he had a grandstand panorama of our previously private courtyard.

Thinking we would do better to sleep in the old kitchen which had been the inhabited quarters of the previous owner, we trooped downstairs again, much subdued and waded through the undergrowth across the courtyard to unlock the door. Inside was the poignant debris of the former occupant's circumscribed village life. During her occupancy it contained a concrete sink over which a small dirty, warped mirror hung by a string; a low single cot; and a few dishes. The large opening of the blackened fireplace was partially covered with peeling oilcloth, and a flash of imagination drew a vignette of an old woman dressed in black bending over her meagre cooking pot on the open fire in the smoke filled room. She was sitting on one of the two broken chairs left in the room and she coughed miserably in the smoke and winter cold before a blink dispersed the vision.

Now thoroughly dejected, we drifted out again opting for higher ground and an attempt to sweep out the last twenty years of dust layering the upstairs room of the main house. We decided that this must be done early to allow the remnants to settle before laying the groundsheet and blowing up our airbeds.

First, though, a drink, let's not look in the shed yet. Alas, there was no water from the solitary outside tap. We turned to each other with transparently feeble smiles trying to put on brave faces.

"What the hell, I'd rather have retsina anyway. Let's go down to the shop."

Thus began the adventure in our new home. Each visit

repeated the same pattern. With trepidation we opened the gate from the lane and surveyed the latest disasters in the decaying structure. Depression set in and lasted about three days, after which a good cleaning and the warmth of the villagers restored our equanimity and sent our hopes soaring for the day when the place might be habitable. We moved around the house considerably, relocating our sleeping quarters to the corner most remote from the current construction work, trying to find spots which didn't leak or rain debris from the flaking ceiling.

On the first few visits to the village we couldn't find any eating establishments and subsisted on salad, cheese and bread. For manual workers, as we had become, this diet was less than satisfactory so we bought a camp stove for simple one pot meals. They were unimaginative and rather boring so we were eventually forced to make a determined effort to find out whether places to eat existed. Our discovery of the unmarked and heavily disguised taverna was one of our greatest early triumphs.

Taking coffee and a beer in the cafenion we managed to convey the message that we were hungry and looking for somewhere to eat. The proprietor pointed down the main road and said "taverna". We elatedly scooted down that street and searched up and down for half an hour, it was filled with private residences, no signs, no taverna. We went back to our less than appetizing home cooked fare. The next night we began our search again, peering into lanes and houses in the dark.

A man getting into his car said, "Deutsch?" (all Cretans seem to assume that any foreigners are German and statistically they will probably be right). We explained in our embryonic Greek that we were from Canada and were looking for the taverna. He pointed along the street in the direction that we had just searched for the second evening running.

We persisted, "Where exactly?"

Taking us by the arm like moronic children he took us to a darkened house and yelled, "Manoli". A few minutes later an amiable figure came to the top of the outside staircase and held a rapid conversation with our guide. Since it was obviously apparent that we still didn't have a clue what was happening we were motioned to wait while the man went back inside the house. He returned with a teenaged girl, who asked in impeccable English, "Can I help you?"

This was our introduction to Eugenia, the tall, sweet-faced, 15 year old daughter of Manolis the Taverna. She explained that this was indeed a taverna, (despite the complete absence of signs, lights or other indications) but it didn't open for another hour or so. We were, however, welcome to wait in the downstairs part of the house, which was in fact the taverna, until they did open. We felt a great surge of relief at meeting this saviour since, not only was our immediate hunger to be satisfied but we had now discovered someone that could help us to communicate with the local population about all the many things we found mysterious and confusing.

That night we had our first taste of Manolis' barbecued "brisoles" (pork chops) accompanied by his wife Maria's superb hand cut chips fried in virgin olive oil. There is no menu, the meal is always pork chops, chips, salad and bread. The only decisions to be made are which type of salad, Greek, cabbage or lettuce, depending on the season, and on whether to drink soft drinks, beer, bottled retsina or local draft wine. They have become very good friends of ours and have helped us out of numerous predicaments, usually precipitated by our lack of language skills or knowledge of local customs.

Eugenia was enthusiastic in extolling the village's virtues. In her excitement she brought out photographs, which included several shots of her playing knee deep in snow in a winter resort. We hadn't realized she was so well travelled and asked, idly, where the photos were taken.

"In the garden, last year," she said.

"Yes, but where?"

She pointed outside the door. "Right here, in the village. And this one is on the street outside. See that house?"

We nearly dropped the photo album in shock. There went our vision of a semi-tropical paradise. We had rejected one village because someone chanced to mention snow. We had accepted this one because no one bothered to mention it. So much for our informed decision-making!

On another early renovation session we received an unexpected phone call from the taverna. Maria, the sister of the previous owner of our house, had turned up there and told Eugenia that she wanted us to go to the police station in Agios Mironas (a nearby village) that morning to sign a paper. A great deal of confusion ensued but we finally worked out that her son, Nikos, who stood to inherit, had heard of the discrepancy between the price we had paid for the house, and the price his aunt had received. It wasn't surprising that he had heard, since the village has an active rumour mill. The not inconsiderable difference between what we had paid and what she had received was made up in taxes, lawyer's fees and a hefty commission to Lawrence, the broker. Eugenia was suffering excruciating embarrassment in her unwilling job as translator in the unpleasant business but was far too courteous to say so.

When we arrived at the taverna Nikos was there with his truck ready to take us to Agios Mironas. The police didn't want to have anything to do with us or with the prepared paper, so we agreed to go back to Kato Asites and got into the truck. Once we were in the truck Nikos announced that we were going to Heraklion. We were being kidnapped. We made two stops enroute, one for fuel (we went from empty to nearly empty) and one for Nikos to have a pee by the roadside while we sat whistling inside the truck.

We circumnavigated Heraklion by the port road and parked illegally by the East gate although it was not clear to us why we could not have parked just as illegally but more conveniently on our side of town. (The parking ticket which was waiting on Nikos' truck would have been just the same price). Then we walked to a lawyer's office in the middle of town and joined a large crowd of clients simultaneously clamouring for his attention. After a few minutes our group got up, went out, walked a block or so, turned around and went back again. We sat down. After a minute we got up again. This time everyone went out - the lawyer, some other people in his office, Nikos, Maria and us. The lawyer descended one floor by the elevator, everyone else took the stairs. The lawyer and his retinue left us outside the law courts while we continued to follow Nikos and Maria, very confused and by this time somewhat annoyed.

Meanwhile we wrote out a statement to append to the Greek document they were hoping we would sign. Our addendum, in English, stated the amount of money that we had paid to the broker for the house. (This amount was much less than the figure Nikos quoted in the document. We haven't a clue where he got his number from but it was a little surprising he hadn't bothered to try to verify it with us, since he had us captive.) We hoped our little English addendum would mitigate our liability for whatever else we would be swearing to. We were still confused about what they hoped to gain from the exercise. We had no idea what they planned to do with their mysterious paper, if they wanted more money and, if so, from whom? We made small talk for half an hour in a rather strained manner to Nikos until the lawyer arrived and then we all went to the nearby police station. A policeman in this town station read the papers prepared by Nikos, with our little addendum. He requested our passports before he would witness our signatures on the documents. We didn't have them with us so we went back home having completely wasted the morning. It was turning out to be a hell of a day for all of us.

Nikos was all for taking us back to the village to collect our passports and straight back to Heraklion again to complete the paperwork. Good old-fashioned exasperation, however, overcame cultural diffidence and we told him (politely) where he could put his truck. We had had enough and reluctantly promised instead that next time we needed to go to town for supplies we would drop in for his errand. This we did, riding to Heraklion on the bus the following week with Maria. We signed the paper, and that was the last we ever heard about it. Throughout all this commotion Maria was constantly courteous and smiling and invited us several times to drop in to her house for coffee. She was and is thus more typical of the village people than her selfish son who wanted to manoeuvre us for his own gain. However, no hard feelings remain on either side and we exchange friendly greetings with Nikos whenever we see him in his fields or in the cafenion.

CHAPTER THREE

Battle with Bureaucracy

THREE

After having our house in Canada up for sale all of one summer and autumn without receiving a single offer we tried again the following January and suddenly we received two good offers at once.

We were so overcome by the prospect that we would suddenly have all our books, files and paraphernalia in the middle of our rather untidy construction site in Crete, that we immediately cancelled all other plans and took off for a two week session on the house. This was also to be our first experience of the house and village in winter. Undaunted we sat in our comfortable living room and prepared a plan. This time we were going to be systematic and start at the top of the house (roofs, ceilings) and repair/clean our way down.

We arrived in Kato Asites after a disastrous journey. There had been storms for over a week so there were no ferries or flights into Heraklion. After our transatlantic and transeuropean flights we were already exhausted and not really in the mood to camp out in Athens airport or delay our return to Crete in any way. We eventually went standby on a flight to Hania, the old capital at the west end of the island. We arrived there late at night, fell into a taxi with all our luggage and ended up at an overpriced noisy hotel next to the bus station. The location proved to be a godsend when we took the morning bus for the three hour ride to Heraklion. From Heraklion we finally took a taxi to our home in the hills.

We arrived at the house at midday. As usual, the "avli", courtyard, was full of litter and leaves, but there were other surprises waiting for us, making us wonder what we were doing here. This arrival would test to the limit the ability of the village to perform its customary magic on us.

Our work plan was our first casualty. The aged window frame in the upstairs window had finally succumbed to the storms and had blown in completely, allowing the rain to soak both the bedroom floor and the downstairs rooms below. There was obvious evidence of rat activity all over the place. A dead cat lay by the toilet (thank god it was the cold season)! Large puddles had formed in the kitchen from leaks in the roof and seepage through the walls where they are below ground level. Apart from that, the house was fine.

After we cleared up this mess we were thoroughly chilled and tried to light the stove. We set up our new wood stove in the main building, removed a pane of glass and stuffed the flue pipe out through the window. Unfortunately, the stove smoked so thoroughly and gave out so little heat that it was utterly defeated by the gale blowing through the missing pane. We moved it into the old kitchen in the hope that it would be able to heat the smaller volume.

Throughout the night we gradually kept stoking the stove and moving our bed closer and closer to it at great risk to ourselves. Paula got so close at one stage that she started melting her acrylic track suit, serving duty as the top stratum of multi-layered pyjamas. At regular intervals we also had to get up, pump up the gradually deflating air bed and try to stem the leaks. Still we were freezing. Each time we woke up during that disturbed night we again wondered why we had bought this wreck on the other side of the world.

Over the next few days the leak in the air bed grew and grew and we landed on the cold floor at ever more frequent intervals during the night. It became a test - do we get up and blow up the bed in the freezing cold in anticipation of another couple of warmer and more comfortable hours sleep, or do we cut our losses and stay snuggled up on the hard cold floor, four blankets underneath us and three blankets on top? There was some pretty serious snuggling going on during that trip and precious little washing! The weather continued wet, windy and cold. It snowed once or twice. The metre thick walls of the house ensured that no warmth or sunlight could penetrate to the rooms.

On Monday night we remembered that rubbish pick up days are Tuesday and Friday. Mike asked Paula, "Did you put the cat out?" Such a macabre inversion of so cosy and domesticated an expression caused the first peels of laughter to ring in the courtyard that trip.

Our departure maintained the general standards of the trip. We got off the overnight ferry in Piraeus and wandered into a local cafe at around 6:30 am. It was filled with assorted old salts all obviously enjoying the only item on the menu, soup. We ordered two large bowls in our impeccable Greek, only able to ascertain that it wasn't fish nor, mysteriously, was it meat. When it came the waiter poured vinegar and pepper on it and left us to enjoy it. We soon found out that it was tripe soup, revolting and effectively inedible to our delicate morning palates. We paid and slunk out to find cheese pies and coffee. We really must step up the Greek lessons, we reminded each other. For future reference, if someone offers us "patsas" soup for breakfast, we'll say no thanks.

Back in Toronto, we began the daunting task of sorting and

packing. We packed 26 boxes of books before we were halted relatively early by the ones we were still using for work and reference. For months we had been making anxious passes of the shelves, goading each other into trying to come up with the most rejects which we were willing to leave behind. After studying each shelf in detail, we came up with two slim books each. Now that we had sold the house, however, we were really motivated. We managed the emotional detachment required to sell or give away three small boxes, mostly old textbooks and very bad novels. Next we had to sort out our office papers. On Sunday mornings between 9 and 11 am we developed the peculiar hobby of watching Coronation Street, drinking sherry and sorting work files.

In the end, we decided to rid ourselves of inessentials like dishes and furniture and keep instead the books and most of the files. Consequently we made a "garage sale" list of our electrical appliances, dining room suite, lawnmower, microwave, other valuables and worthless junk. With two kids just out of university, it seemed only fair to give them first refusal of items on the list. They immediately carted off everything of value to their respective apartments.

We received Paula's father's expert advice on whether strollers in the neighbourhood would be sufficiently interested in old textbooks to warrant a garage sale. Her father and mother came over for the weekend and helped pack and organize the disposal of the remaining items. These included such treasures as dog-eared reproductions of paintings and assorted mis-matched knick-knacks. The very bad novels sold like hot cakes. Months later in Crete we would say to each other, "Where did that thingamajig go?" "Sold it." Then we went out and bought another one.

In this way we got the contents of our Canadian house down to manageable proportions and booked a moving company. The day before moving day a 20 foot long container was driven up and parked in our drive. Early the next morning the packing/loading team arrived and started dismantling and wrapping items, including the new kitchen cabinets in their cardboard boxes, a bath/shower stall, our used washing machine, a ten foot long wall map of the world and our two ancient bicycles. After about four hours the container was loaded and the wooden braces, to hold the load steady, were nailed into position. The container was locked and sealed and we treated the team to a lunch of beer and Kentucky Fried Chicken. Four weeks later we flew off to Crete to get the house ready to receive this consignment.

We had been warned by other expats that owning a house in Crete is tantamount to running a free hotel for relatives and friends you never knew you had and although there is perhaps an element of truth in this, there is also a positive side. We look forward to the arrival of visitors. It gives us a chance to explore Crete with our friends and speak freely about complicated topics without language difficulties.

Our first visitors were total strangers and they arrived before we had received that container from Canada with all our worldly goods, including niceties like beds and chairs. They were John and Diana from Vancouver, both New Zealanders originally, and they had been given our address by an ex-colleague of Mike's. They called from the village square early one sunny afternoon and we went to bring them to the house. After showing them around our cosy construction site and dumping their bags we went for a few beers at Niko's cafeteria. With the first two rounds, Nikos brought us some nuts. For the third, he popped over the road to his garden plot and plucked some tiny artichokes which he served us raw, quartered and sprinkled with salt and lemon. They were delicious. We had a few more beers and when we had had more than enough Niko crowned them with an ouzo on the house. A sobering walk was in order so we strolled a half kilometre to Ano Asites where we had another beer. Refreshed, we went to the taverna and had some wine before and during dinner. At the end of dinner Manolis the Mechanic came in and started an enthusiastic flurry of "aspro pato" (bottom's up).

Mike manfully matched him drink for drink but Manolis had no idea of the head start Mike had had. After honour was served, we thought we could finally extricate ourselves and stood up to leave. Mike righted himself with no problem. Then, as we watched in bewilderment, his legs seemed to melt and he slowly shrank, becoming shorter and smaller, just like the Wicked Witch of the West. With an apologetic, lopsided grin he passed out and had to be carried home. Fortunately John is a large ex-rugby player, so having helped Mike get in that condition, he was able to assist in getting him out of it.

The gossip had spread round the whole village by early the next morning and Mike was offered temperance advice at every opportunity. John and Diana slept on our air beds which we knew would self deflate in about two hours, giving them the option of trying to sleep on the cold, hard floor, or getting up and pumping them up again. After the night before, however, they got up the next morning remarkably refreshed, saying they hadn't noticed a thing wrong with their "bed". John was so eager to demonstrate how frisky he was he did some of the solder joints for our hot water system. We couldn't test them at the time since the rest of the system was incomplete. Subsequently one awkward elbow joint at the low point of the system leaked, a typical example of hangover plumbing.

The Kiwis introduced us to the word "TABEPNA", which is how the Greek word taverna looks if you ignore the fact that a different alphabet is in use. We introduced them to the concept of different coloured drinking vouchers, currency notes. After several lively evenings and as many slow mornings we saw John and Diana off for a tour of the island with lunch at our favourite port restaurant.

The arrival of our goods snug in their own container after an eight week voyage was quite an event. A number of phone calls between shipping agents, customs officials and the Canadian company that we had supposedly paid to do all this, finally determined a date for the container's arrival in Heraklion. We rented a car and drove into town early since we were told that we had to clear customs first thing in the morning. It was a slow business. The customs agent was expecting us to have some idea of the whereabouts of our goods or the lorry driver but we didn't have a single clue. Helplessly, we handed over all our papers in the hope they might be able to glean more information from them than we could. Finally, they phoned up some of the larger moving companies and located our man. Then we spent several hours wandering around the customs office waiting for things we didn't understand and showing our lists of goods to sundry officials. Finally, we got to the stage where someone had located the container and appointed an inspector who wanted to go and see it.

So did we! We formed the end of a convoy consisting of the custom's inspector, the truck driver and us and drove the few hundred metres to the bonded customs enclosure. This was difficult to identify since it seemed to occupy the same space as the car park for the ferry terminal.

Having confirmed that it was the correct container the truck driver looked in the documentation for the key to open the seals placed on the container doors in Canada. No keys. The truck driver and the customs man started searching for likely implements to break open the seals. Eventually using a lot of brute force and very little ingenuity they managed to smash the seals and reveal all our worldly goods still snug in their box. The customs men thought we were excessive in our relief but they didn't know we had not taken out insurance for the shipment!

The first thing to catch the custom mans' eye was an empty beer bottle taped to the wooden struts by the Canadian packers. He seemed to think this was a good joke but started getting serious by asking us where we were intending to unload all this stuff so that he could inspect it. We explained that we didn't plan on doing that and since the container wasn't completely full couldn't he inspect it in situ? Much ruffled feathers until we climbed into the container and removed the braces holding the load in place. He then reluctantly agreed that he could see some of the boxes and wanted to know which ones contained electrical goods. These items were, of course, spread throughout the load since we didn't know that electrical goods (and a car which luckily we didn't bring) were the only things they would be interested in. Wouldn't he like to see some lovely books?

He commanded us to open the boxes and show him the contents, particularly any electrical items we could dig out. The container, standing in the sun, was like an oven but we tried to appear cooperative. Mike hiked himself up into the sauna and started pulling out random items to show the inspector, who showed no inclination at all to get up himself and look. He seemed especially pleased when we triumphantly located a small electrical blender. Mike and I chattered away in English, discussing openly what bits of scientific equipment he had unearthed that he wondered whether it would be better to leave hidden. There was nothing wrong with them, but they might be very difficult to explain.

After a while the inspector got bored and signalled us to stop taking things out of the boxes but merely to open the boxes so that it would appear they had been inspected. This new phase continued for another half an hour or so until even he, in the shade at the back of the container was getting quite hot and sweaty. "That'll do", he said, "come back to the office". Mike poured himself soaking wet out of the oven and shook himself like a retriever after a swim. The truck driver closed the doors of the container and accompanied us back to the customs office for the reckoning of duty payable.

There followed another game of following various officials carrying pieces of paper and much scrutiny of our shipping lists. Relying exclusively on our list, our customs agent came up with a number for the duty payable, based largely on the electrical items he had not seen. We followed him to the big boss who studied all the papers carefully and decided that the duty was too low. He did so apparently on the basis that, being immigrants, we would get it all back anyway so it didn't matter how much we were charged. He was utterly charming as he pulled an arbitrary figure out of thin air, roughly three times the calculated duty. The process of getting it back proved to be a saga that rivalled the Odyssey in time and complexity.

We were by now too wet, too anxious to get home and too helpless to argue, so we paid. Ordeal by sauna and we were bested by the old technique of disarming us with a smile. Payment of the duty enabled us to get a stack of papers stamped, papers which we were told would be necessary to take our things out of the "customs area" of the port. We then followed a new truck driver back to the container. He immediately hitched up his rig and headed out of the port via the back entrance. We followed in our rental car still clutching our vital customs clearance papers that had cost us so much time, effort and money and sailed out of the port after the speeding truck without further scrutiny. We headed towards Kato Asites at a fair speed, looking over our shoulders for pursuing customs agents or police.

Arriving at the village we directed the driver to the square where he parked and opened the doors of the container. That was the sum total of his further involvement, all he wanted now was for us to empty the container in plenty of time for him to return to Heraklion to catch the evening ferry back to Piraeus. If he was delayed and he didn't make it we would be responsible for heavy daily charges for him, his truck and the container.

What now? we thought. We had all this stuff and our house was the best part of a kilometre away up tiny streets. We thought wildly of several thousand trips with our wheelbarrow but even then a number of the items were too big for that approach.

As in all cases when we didn't know how to tackle a problem, we went down to Manolis the Taverna. It was now around 1 o'clock and we found Manolis and family eating lunch prior to their siesta. After ascertaining from our panicked faces that we couldn't join them for lunch first and then tackle our problem, he cheerfully put down his knife and fork, told us to wait by the container and disappeared into the village, deserted at this time of day. Some ten minutes later, just as in the movies when the sound of bugles announces the arrival of the cavalry to the rescue, we heard the phut phut sound of a mechani (the three wheeled, two-stroke farm vehicle) coming down the street. This was driven by "Bottoms up" Manolis (the Mechanic) with his usual grin. He parked by the container at about the same time as other helpers arrived on foot. Many of these we had never seen before but they got stuck in to unloading the container. A few minutes later the mechani of Michalis our neighbour rolled up closely followed by another driven by another Michalis, a total stranger to us at the time. By now we had about ten helpers plus a number of onlookers.

Manolis the Taverna soon sorted us out into two teams, one at the container unloading and stacking the mechanis nominally being directed by Mike, with the other team under similarly nominal control of Paula at the house. The maze of mechanis (a fair collective noun for machines made by the "Minotaur" company) soon set up a traffic flow pattern that would be the envy of any city urban planning department and the pile of goods in the container slowly but steadily was being reduced. The team at the house was placing boxes, bikes, baths, and other sundry items including our dozens of cartons of fold-flat kitchen cabinets (some assembly required) into their correct locations. They struggled manfully with heavy filing cabinets of papers up the narrow, steep stairs. Many comments were made on the fact that most of our possessions were boxes of books. "Have you read them all? Why do you need so many?"

In an hour we had done it, with a not inconsiderable amount of help from our friends. Some of them accepted a cold drink, no one would accept any money even for fuel for the mechanis. They all disappeared with a deprecatory wave and left us to our pile of stuff and monumental sorting out project. Only one young lad was left. Michalis from across the lane tried to get him out of the yard but he wouldn't budge and Michalis finally had to give up and go home. Then we discovered what the boy wanted. Money. We offered him some but he said that wouldn't be enough so he tripled it. We paid without demure and with a sly, victorious grin he left. He was happy, we were happy. Without the villager's help, and the trusty mechanis, the only vehicles that can approach our house, the whole venture would have been impossible.

With impeccable timing John and Diana returned from a tour of the island the day after our goods arrived. We didn't hold a grudge and spoiled them with a real sprung mattress on the floor, luxury. They had bought Mike a Cretan walking stick for making the difficult journey uphill home from late-night taverna sessions. In another couple of very pleasant days they were liberated of additional drinking vouchers and dragged us off to our very first visit to the Cretan seaside, declaring that we were more than a little bonkers if we had been in Crete on and off for two years without once having been in the sea. Although we couldn't find bathing suits, which were still packed under a mountain of baggage, we ceremoniously dipped our toes in the Cretan Sea before retreating out of the sun to a "tabepna" for a cool beer. Despite the primitive accommodation our first visitors must have liked it, they returned a year later. The ex-pats were right, these visitors were friends we didn't know we had.

A few months later we tried to sort out the paperwork involved with our import of goods into Greece, in order to recover some of the duty we had paid. For this we had to go to Athens, taking the overnight ferry from Heraklion and travelling in from Piraeus with the early morning commuters on the Metro. Emerging at Omonia, we walked up towards Syntagma Square and had coffee and stale rolls in a coffee house. In the Plaka an organ grinder was entertaining the commuters trudging to work. Fresh raisins from Corinth were on sale from early morning street carts. We wandered around the market buying herbs, spices, seeds and a snazzy stainless steel olive oil pourer, then made our way back to the Syntagma area in time for the office opening.

We asked for directions from the information bureau and arrived at the office of foreigners at just before 10:30 and found someone who had our file. A miracle. She studied everything in the file studiously, together with our passports and residency permits. She then wrote almost a page of stuff in each of our passports and stamped the appropriate pages.

After this she directed us elsewhere but since we did not understand she called in an English speaker who explained that we had to go to another office to pay for the inevitable stamps to make the documents legal. She also explained that we didn't need to come back to that office again, which we carefully confirmed by asking three times.

Arriving at the next office, a converted hotel several streets away, we went through the same procedure with a new lady who wrote out what seemed to be a bill for the stamps. With some difficulty we ascertained that we couldn't buy them there but had to go to another office. We asked for directions to this new office but she didn't understand maps so wrote us instructions in Greek. This was not much help so we found another English speaking, map-literate lady who showed us where the next office was, at the other end of the city. She also explained that we didn't need to come back to that office again.

The novelty of this Kafkaesque procedure was beginning to wear thin and it was now getting hot and fumy as only Athens can. We wandered off to the next office and went to the cashier who sent us to another man on the other side of the office. He read everything and wrote out what seemed to be another bill and directed us back to the cashier who now happily took our money, 3210 Drx.

This elaborate procedure for paying stamp duty, we later learned, is an innovation caused by the devaluation of the Greek drachma. Since the duty stamps are still issued in tiny denominations, relatively large amounts of duty would smother the entire document. Hence, a separate bill and receipt are now required. It is well beyond us to ask why they don't simply issue stamps in larger denominations.

The man behind the desk now told us we had to go back to the first office. We debated just going for a beer and forgetting the whole thing but we had lost confidence in our assurance that the other offices said they were finished with us. In the bewildering confusion of Greek bureaucracy, we are never sure who really knows the correct procedures. Which one of several conflicting bits of information do we believe? We pictured ourselves being forced to make another trip to Athens in the future for some final flourish on our paperwork. The cost of making another trip to Athens would completely wipe out the gain in funds achieved by retrieving our duty, leaving us exactly where we started, apart from detailed unwanted knowledge of Greek customs offices. In the end we found ourselves traipsing back across Athens to the very first office. Here we were assured that we didn't need to be there and should now return to the customs office in Heraklion. We finally took our hot, exhausted bodies off for a drink. Bureaucracy was giving us an inordinate fondness for beer.

We caught the overnight ferry back to Heraklion, went straight to the customs office, and announced our successful completion of the papers to the boss. After a depressingly cursory examination of them he took us to his assistant, Maria, who anxiously checked and re-checked our passports, documents from Athens and residency permits. She looked through everything again, wrote on the file, stamped our file (which was now an inch thick). She attached a small slip of paper to the top with a straight pin from her desk. This took two attempts since the first one bent. From our new, hard won experience we have ascertained that straight pins are a major budget item in Greek bureaucracy and septicemia a major occupational hazard.

Maria and our whole file passed up and down the length of the customs office several times. People were, as usual, standing, sitting, gossiping, reading newspapers. It is said that there are three people employed for every government job in Greece. We are prepared to believe it. Maria finally shouted several times for Manolis, "is he here today?" She was assured he would make an appearance. We were instructed to wait for him in front of another, empty desk along the long counter typical of Greek government offices. He arrived shortly and turned out to be none other than our conscientious inspector of goods. He, equally carefully, removed the small slip of paper pinned to the file by Maria and wrote in Mike's passport. After a mere two trips up and down the length of the office he ushered us into the cashier's office where he handed the file to one of two men sitting around and engaged in a lengthy discussion, apparently about what they were to do with it. We bought 400 Drx worth of stamps for 480 Drx and were asked to sign another paper, which turned out to be a receipt. Imagine our amazement when they counted out and gave us back that carefully calculated duty that we had originally paid (minus a processing fee, of course). The fact that it had cost us half the total amount to go to Athens and back and had taken a days of effort did somewhat dampen our feeling of triumph. Still, the main thing was it was over!

CHAPTER FOUR

Constructing a Dream from a Wreck

Although only about 200 years old, our house dates from the stone age. Archaeologists digging beneath the central court at Knossos have unearthed a house dating from the early Neolithic period in Crete, some 7 500 years ago. J.D. Evans described it in 1994 in "Knossos: A Labyrinth of History", thus: "... a great deal of stone, including old quernstones, was incorporated. The eastern and western walls had separate inner and outer faces with a filling of broken bricks and stones between."

Just such a house was our new home, built of two rows of undressed stone filled with rubble in the same manner, with walls more than a metre thick. When we first acquired it it could hardly be described as a "desirable residence". The main building has two large rooms downstairs with a flat concrete roof above the front room. The single, second storey room over the back room has a wooden ceiling under a pitched ceramic tiled roof. This building had been largely abandoned for a number of years, apart from the back section where the animals were kept on the dirt floor.

Across the courtyard is the small old kitchen. The third building, the "apothiki" (storage shed) we later learned, used to be the village olive press and still contained the fireplace where the water was heated for thermal stripping of the oil. The olive press had been replaced by a wine vat. Around the courtyard was a well, filled with rubbish, a collapsing domed oven and, of course, the unplumbed toilet. Just alongside the gate was a single tap, the only water supply to the property.

The old kitchen and the main room of the house had plain concrete floors, the upstairs room had a wooden floor made from boards (probably cypress) some 40 cm wide and the floors of the apothiki and back room were packed earth. All of the roofs leaked, to a lesser or greater extent. Many of the walls had holes in them, which proved to be rat access points. Most of the windows had panes of glass missing and rotting frames. The back room had no window, merely a board nailed over an opening in the wall.

There was an electrical supply to the house. This consisted of a single circuit with the 5 Amp fuse replaced by an old copper Greek drachma. This circuit gave a single light to each of the rooms, but we never dared use it since the fuse box and most of the light cords were running with water. At a crucial juncture of our electrical investigations we discovered with a shock (literally!) that the electricity supply had never been cut off, although the house had been unoccupied for years.

It was difficult to decide where to begin. The building was a shell and we had to design kitchen, bathroom, bedrooms and library and locate water and sewage pipes, wiring, light fixtures and power points. We set about measuring everything, planning layouts, making priority lists of tasks, equipment and supplies that we would need. We made methodical timetables of work for each of our visits, with starting and completion dates. When we arrived to start work we threw them out and fixed the things that were in most danger of falling down or blowing up.

In the initial stages of our restoration work we were bringing many of our tools and some of the supplies from North

America on our frequent trips. There were many supplies that we had to obtain locally though, since the airlines do not like transporting many tonnes of cement, sand, lengths of wood, etc., at least, not without a large premium. It was a major struggle to find sources of many of the things we needed since in many cases we did not even know the correct name in English let alone in Greek. We very soon discovered that most things to do with building, plumbing, electrical work, etc., are not available in the village and must be bought in Heraklion.

Many of our first tasks involved making concrete so we required large quantities of sand, gravel and cement. This was one of the easier supply problems to solve, the yards carrying this sort of products are, by their nature, pretty obvious and it is not too difficult to drive a rental car up to the appropriate pile and point. Things like 1/2 inch copper elbows, electrical breakers and quarter round trim needed a bit more persistence. We had purchased an English-Greek technical dictionary which gave us a start and we had a lucky break when we discovered a hardware store in Heraklion that sold many essentials. We soon became regular customers. Since the owner of the store had spent some time in Vancouver he spoke a little English and could help us locate the more obscure items that he didn't stock. It was a matter of necessity, not pride, for us to keep English to an absolute minimum and to get along exclusively in Greek.

We explored all the back streets and holes in the wall in the working sections of Heraklion town, finding small electrical shops and equipment stores. It was only when we had finished most of the major renovation work that we discovered

Gotzen. Gotzen is a large, self-service, Do It Yourself shop near the bus station in Heraklion that sold virtually everything that we had expended so much effort in finding. Just the sort of shop we daily wished for, "Why isn't there a Canadian Tire store when you really need it?" We might as well have said, "I wish there were a Gotzen."

Since our lane is too narrow for cars to negotiate, our supplies have all had to be dumped at the corner below us, some 100 metres away and carted up the steep hill. One of our first purchases, and one of our most used items, was a wheelbarrow. We dumped sacks of sand, wooden planks, lengths of copper pipe, etc., into the barrow and hauled the booty up to the house.

On one occasion when we needed to transport a bathroom fixture too large for a car and we also wanted a lot of sand and gravel, we learned how to hire a 5 ton lorry. The system for such rentals is easy, once you know it. There are a number of such goods lorries parked by the Heraklion city wall, near the Hania Gate. The drivers are in one of the nearby cafenia (the plural of cafenion). You hover around one of these trucks until someone spots you and comes along or, if you feel more pro-active, you go to the cafenion and ask for a truck. Once you have negotiated the price for where you want to go the truck and driver are yours until you've finished moving whatever you wish to move.

Having selected our lorry we picked up the bathroom fixture first then went to the sand and gravel yard. The lorry driver lamented the extra cost of buying sand and gravel in convenient sacks and convinced us that for the same price we could fill his whole lorry with a loose load. With a great deal of trepidation we let ourselves be persuaded. We took out the bathroom fixture, filled the lorry with the correct mix of sand and gravel, then re-loaded the cabinet precariously on top. Arriving as close to our house as possible we man-handled down the bathroom unit and struggled with it up to the house.

In the meantime the truck driver backed into the narrow lane used for parking access by two of our neighbours and for turning around by most of the rest of the village. He also backed into the small general store on one side and an abandoned house on another. When we came hurrying down the hill with our wheel barrow we were just in time to see him tipping the last of the load of sand and gravel into the road and he was ready to be paid and return to Heraklion. Alright for him, he made his getaway, but what were we to do with an obstructing mountain and several cars probably clambering to get down that lane? We started slowly to dig our way into it and move it with our puny wheelbarrow up to the house where we piled it up in the middle of the courtyard.

Luckily one of our neighbours, Giorgos, whom we had not met previously, saw our plight and took pity on us. He went and collected his mechani, brought it to our sand pile and started shovelling sand and gravel into the back of his vehicle. A few trips with the trusty mechani and we moved what would have taken us hours without his help. When we finished he quietly drove off, almost before we could thank him.

One of our first priorities was to provide an indoor toilet to replace the open-air version which came with the house. We concreted a small slab under the stairs in the back room and cemented in the toilet. We connected the sewage pipe and laid it across the front room, through the wall and out under the flower beds, carefully calculating distances and slopes. We then came to the point of having to remove the old toilet and make the connection to the town sewers. Of necessity this job had to be done speedily. Once we had committed and removed the old toilet we were without facilities until we connected the new one. We were a little puzzled by the fact that we couldn't find the position of the connection to the sewage system. There was nothing coming out of the back of the toilet and on the side visibility was obscured by a mysterious hump of concrete. Before tackling the job we tried to guess the plumbing details. Finally we decided we would just have to start dismantling and play it by ear.

Our first clue that we had a problem was when Paula, excavating the last part of the trench for our new pipe, observed that there were a lot of worms in the soil. When we lifted the old toilet we found out why. The outlet from the toilet drained or plopped out of the side and, together with rain water from the yard, all leaked and flowed along a crude stone and rubble channel roughly in the direction of the open end of the pipe leading to the town sewer. Most of the contents of the outlet were percolating into the yard and down into the shed. When we plucked up courage to tackle the shed we found a large pile of rubbish on the other side of the wall immediately behind the toilet, which was saturated with waste from the toilet and the used toilet paper that had been thrown over the wall. A description of this work has put off many of our visitors dreaming romantically of renovating their own Cretan home.

To make our spiffy new toilet completely functional we needed to supply a constant source of water to it. Since the village water supply is intermittent everyone in the village has a water storage tank, which provides back-up when the village supply is off. We had now arrived at the stage when we needed just such a back-up. We had spotted a workshop in Heraklion with a number of these galvanised steel tanks being manufactured by a one man operation. Parking our rental car outside we explained that we wanted one of the 1 metre cubes. He offered us one just being completed and explained the price to us. After we paid he tried to ascertain how we were planning to remove it from his shop and transport it the twenty odd kilometres to Kato Asites. We indicated that we were planning to use the tiny Fiat soft top car. His laugh broke off abruptly once he had grasped that we were serious. "Panagia mou (Mother of God)". He helped us lift it on to the top of the car and tie it in place with the rope we had brought with us for this purpose. With much shaking of his head and muttering he saw us climb in through the car windows and drive out into the Heraklion traffic.

Luckily it was a day completely without wind and we made an uneventful journey, although we got some stares from the cafenion crowd as we drove through the square. Arriving at our nearest unloading spot we dropped the tank off the car roof, unharmed, and manhandled it up the street and straight up on to our flat roof. On our next visit to town we went to the water tank workshop to reassure him that we had made it safely with our cargo. Smiles all round. Now we had the luxury of a constant supply of cold water from our one outdoor tap and to our indoor toilet.

The next day we were trying to decide whether to start fitting the new concrete lintels that we had made to replace the rotten wooden ones above the upstairs bedroom window, or start the nasty job of cementing in the waste pipe connection to the mains sewage. Going upstairs to investigate the lintels, we soon committed ourselves willy nilly. The stones, wood and clay were all so unstable and rotten that the whole lot started to come down whenever we touched anything. There were two very large stones precariously perched on top of the old rotten lintels. Paula went downstairs to fetch tools while Mike was on the ladder clearing the debris. With an almighty crash one of the large boulders fell. Paula frantically tore back up upstairs, screaming for Mike. His leg was bleeding where the falling rock had grazed it. After a moment he said that he was alright but Paula was so frightened that she cried and needed many hugs before calming down. The larger boulder, an immense rock, was still in position and it seemed to be hanging in midair. We knew that we would be unable to lift it down and back up safely and if it came down unaided it would have gone right through the wooden floor.

Paula was shaking with fright when we lifted the first lintel. It wouldn't go in, there was not enough room under the big rock. As we were trying to manoeuvre it the ladder tipped away and Mike fell, dropping his end. As if in slow motion the lintel and mortar came down. Desperately clinging to it as long as possible to give Mike time to get away, it seemed an age to Paula as Mike's end slowly dropped, breaking the base of the window ledge, slowly sinking to the platform and floor. Mike was not injured but, again, we were both quite shaken. It was a near miss.

We took a break while we rested and tried to work out what

to do next. Trying to shave chips off a lower rock started the large one trembling again so we thought we must try to wedge it up out of the way. We nailed some timbers together for extra strength and tried to lever the end up. It stuck on the cracked window sill. After some time we tried again and the rock pivoted and turned so that it was lower and we were worse off than when we started. It was even shakier and less secure than before and every touch seemed to weaken the rotten lintel further.

Finally Mike suggested that Paula wedge the support under the rock while he lifted it up with his shoulder. This meant that she had to stand directly under the boulder while Mike blocked her escape route. We were terrified but could think of no other method. We screwed up our courage and tried it. It worked!

The rock was now much more stable and there seemed to be enough clearance for the lintel if we placed the opposite end in first at an angle. This left Mike with the complicated manoeuvre of lifting the rock to loosen the support beam, which was now in the way, and simultaneously fit the rock end of the lintel. The far end went in easily but the end under the rock was only resting precariously on the rounded shoulder of the window surround. He tipped the rock and the support prop fell loose. We snatched it out of the way and the beam was in. Now by barring up the rock a bit at a time we could push the lintel into a more secure position.

The first lintel was up. More hugs and a break for lunch. We were both weak and tired, both from tension and from physical work.

We debated leaving it at that for the day but after a substantial lunch and some liquid courage we decided to attempt the other two lintels. They were tricky because we had the delicate task of balancing the rock on the one new lintel while we tried to get the others in.

We worked from outside this time, breaking away an old, unsuccessful repair job and rotten concrete. Behind it was an apparently solid wooden lintel and mortared stones in a curved arch which clearly showed where the old repair work had been done. The apparently sound beam too was rotten and shook at a touch. When we removed it we could see that it was reduced to less than a third of its original 10 cm thickness.

The whole surround had to be disassembled rock by rock, leaving a gaping hole in the wall right up to the roof and committing us to a complete repair now. After excavating a space for the second lintel we wedged up the large rock on the existing middle lintel beam (a log), the soundest of the three. There were lots of larvae of wood-eating bugs everywhere so the good wood would not have lasted much longer. Much of the mortar was still wet from many soakings by rain. No cement had been used at all in constructing the wall; only rocks and mud.

After we had supported the rock and moved the platform (four cinder blocks and a paving slab) around to the outside we were ready for the second lintel. We used the same technique of moving it up the ladder steps one at a time and then Mike used his shoulder to carry it up the rest of the way. It was comparatively easy and went in without difficulty.

Lastly we had to move the inside lintel to the centre and fit another behind it. To do this we once again had to support the large rock with the prop but by now we had worked out a workable procedure.

Paula became over confident and didn't use the paving stone platform this time as it was heavy and a nuisance to move. It was a mistake, the extra centimetres of height had helped and lifting was now very awkward. In addition, the cinder blocks on which she stood were out of position so she had to hold one end of the lintel on the ladder while Mike came down and moved them. Nevertheless, we finally did it, all three lintels were up.

Although by now it was quite late and we were both tired we decided to try to cement everything in while we were still flushed with success and so we mixed a load of sand and cement. Just as we were beginning this job Mike started a migraine and had to take his pills and rest. Paula levelled the outside lintel since the cement was mixed already and after too few minutes Mike came back and we finished, unscathed, the most dangerous construction job in the house.

Having completed some of the more urgent repair jobs we decided to tackle the apothiki to make space for storing tools, supplies and equipment. We collected a great stack of old straw, wood, paper, etc., and decided to burn it. Also in the shed was a 50 gallon drum which had a dark substance lining the inside but looked ideal as a container for our bonfire. We set it up in the yard one night and tried to light the first load of rubbish. We achieved a courtyard filled with chokingly acrid smoke. Barely able to see each other, coughing and eyes streaming we persevered, using paraffin and our plumbing blow torch we managed to get some semblance of flame in the acrid smoke. Kids were shouting and playing in the street outside but we weren't in the mood for visitors so we kept the gate shut. Eventually it dawned on us that the shouts were unusually frantic. As we flung open the gate we caught a glimpse of the astonished, staring face of our neighbour, Yannis the Bulldozer. He stopped dead in the act of shouting to one of his sons who was struggling up the street with a ladder. He was about to scale our garden wall.

They had smelled the acrid smoke, hardly surprising since we had filled the village with it, and seen the sparks and glow from our attempt at combustion. He had seen no other lights (this was before we had electricity and we were using only candles and torches). No one had responded to his urgent shouts, (we didn't know the words for FIRE! HELP! and hadn't understood a thing). Thinking that the burning house was deserted, the volunteer firefighters were just at the point of effecting a dramatic rescue when we casually opened our gate. We rather shamefacedly apologized, thanked them and poured water on our precious fire. "No no", they said, "no problem, carry on with your rubbish disposal". But we didn't dare. We merely put all the rubbish back in the shed and it went to the tip months later when Michalis helped us remove all the other debris from there. Yannis used the occasion to have a look around the house and kindly forgave us our serious social gaff. The house, yard and shed stank for weeks.

CHAPTER FIVE

Cafenia, Camaraderie and Kleptocrats

Crete is a place renowned for the sophistication and beauty of its 90 or 100 cosmopolitan cities - more than two thousand years ago! It is has a smaller population now than it did then. Cretans have ancestors who had every right to call the war-loving Myceneans and classical Athenians crude upstarts and copycat bumpkins; Minoans were treated with solemn respect by the Pharaohs of Egypt's Middle Kingdom. One of the most ancient civilizations of the world, it gave to Greece and Europe winemaking, dance and song, the technique of pressing olives for oil and the first written Greek. Although it has known scarcely a day without domination by a succession of invaders, Cretans staunchly maintain a well-earned reputation for fierce independence. Mainland Greeks proclaim Cretans to be untrustworthy and unpredictable but laud them for their prodigious hospitality to strangers. They have been called liars due to a misunderstanding by one of their conquerors of antiquity - who stole a minor god sacrificed annually in order to ensure fertility of the earth, turned him into Zeus, king of gods, and declared him immortal. They then declared Cretans liars for pointing out the burial place of the Cretan Zeus, since Zeus, they claimed, was immortal. The libel was perpetuated in the bible by Paul and immortalized in a logical conundrum - "All Cretans are liars. I am a liar."

Crete, "The Great Island", at 260 km long and from 12 to 56 km wide is the fifth largest island in the Mediterranean and the largest in Greece. It has been continuously inhabited since the Neolithic period, at least 8 000 years. It has had many names over the centuries including: Aeria, for its mild climate; Chthonia, for its size or for the goddess Demetra also known as Chthonia and worshipped in Crete; Dolichi, for its oblong shape; Telchinia, by the Telchines who were among Crete's earliest inhabitants; Idea, from Mount Idi or the Nymph (Idean); Makaris, land of bliss for its fertile and productive soil; Kouretis, land of the Koures that is of youths, valiant lads; and Crete, from the Nymph Crete, or from Creta son of Jupiter, and its reputed ancient King.

The occupiers of Crete have included the Myceneans, Dorians, Romans, Saracen Arabs, Venetians and Turks with the most recent being the oppressive presence of the German Army in World War II. It is only in very recent times, 1913, that Crete became part of Greece and the Cretans still see themselves as a race apart.

An encyclopedia of 1881-5 records that: "(Crete) contains extensive woods, pastures and meadows and produces corn, wine, oil, opium, liquorice, flax, cotton, silk, carobs, oranges, lemons, dates, and other southern produce." Opium as a major crop is something that doesn't get much mention in guide books of today, although wild poppies are still abundant. The carob tree is still grown in Crete and used mostly for animal fodder although small amounts are exported for the health food market as a chocolate substitute. It was also used to provide a cellulose gum used in curing tobacco and for photographic products and paper-making. The little horn shaped bean, the keraton, was used by the ancient Greeks as a standard measure for gold and precious stones, the origin of the carat. It was not a very reliable standard, beans may vary in weight by about 20%. Carobs are also known as St. John's Bread, as the baptist is thought to have survived in the wilderness by eating them.

The old encyclopedia also claimed that there were about 600,000 sheep and goats with about 50,000 horned cattle, used chiefly for ploughing. The population, according to an estimate made in 1877, was 227,933, of whom 132,400 (only 58%) were Greeks. That is more than two sheep for every person, of any race, on the island.

Cretans still consider themselves a separate identity from the rest of Greece and we have been told by the villagers themselves that they have much more in common with Egypt and Anatolia (which is now Turkey, although you could never drag that out of the Greeks) than with people from Macedonia or Salonika. People here think of themselves as Eastern. "We are," they said, "as different from northern Greeks as we are from Americans."

The standard of comfort and modernity in village homes varies considerably. At one extreme are the homes of many old people whom we have visited. Inside, many are the original plastered rough stonework that ours was when we first bought it. These houses have no electricity and a solitary water tap just inside the gate. They cook on a two-burner camp stove with bottled gas or on an open fire. At night olive oil lamps provide illumination and, instead of a fridge, food is put into a container and lowered down into the cool water of the well in the courtyard. Often these old people live in one downstairs room when they become too feeble to tackle the steep stairs.

At the other extreme some of the village houses have been

built in very modern style, from cinder blocks instead of stone, which have much less insulating capacity, so do not stay cool in summer or (comparatively) warm in winter. These homes are fitted with electric ranges, fridges, washing machines, central heating, food-processors, etc. Interior decorating is done with marble, ceramic, wood and fabrics.

All the elegance of a Cretan home is lavished on the formal parlour, all the comfort and practicality on the kitchen. Embroidery covers every horizontal surface. From an early age girls are taught needlework and start to replicate the ancient patterns used to make the tablecloths, antimacassars, doilies and pillow cases that will form the basis of their "bottom drawer". Women spend all their spare time, particularly during the winter, on this craft. On warm days they sit outside in small groups, facing the wall, chatting while they prepare these items for their daughter's wedding.

Bedrooms are spartan and functional, sometimes reduced to a mere bed in the corner. People sleep in clothes, under blankets without sheets. The blankets are taken out to air almost every fine day. Most houses also have an outbuilding for storage of fuel and for keeping chickens, rabbits and goats. These buildings are sometimes completely detached from the living quarters and may be down the road or across the lane. Thus, old Yannis the Widower can claim to have four "houses" in the village although they should more accurately be described as sheds (including the one he lives in).

The first thing you notice when you enter a Cretan home is your welcome. Your host begs you to enter and before you know it you are seated round the huge kitchen table which is the central feature of the house. There is always room for one more and chairs enough for a horde are usually stored around the walls and in every spare corner. The rooms are always kept meticulously clean and a Cretan housewife would probably die of embarrassment if a visitor saw her floor unscrubbed or her pots dirty. Smells are crucially important. We know several women who do most of their cooking outside or in another building, especially fish or strongly scented dishes. One family won't eat cauliflower, not because they don't like it but because it stinks while it is boiling. What they must think of our house, with its curries and Chinese and garlic smells!

Every housewife, even those with the most up to date electric cooker, still keeps a small gas burner to make coffee. Even as she is spooning the coffee into the traditional, long-handled pot, she is asking how much sugar and reaching for the traditional spoon sweet.

Unlike so many Greek villages, Kato Asites is not a dying community, with a few black clad widows and decrepit men lingering among the abandoned and derelict houses. It has a population of about 2 000 people and there is both a small nursery school and a primary school with eight teachers and 120 students ranging in age from 5 to 12 years. After this, children either leave school completely or go on to the high school at Agios Mironas, which is about five kilometres away and is the administrative centre of the Maleveziou district with a post office, police station and telephone office.

Apart from the regular school, Kato Asites also has an evening school which teaches foreign languages, mainly

German and English to fee-paying junior pupils. In the main square there is a bakery which every day, except Sunday, bakes fresh white and black bread, sweet sesame buns and bread rusks, which are soaked in milk or water before eating. The circular loaves used by the church for their numerous religious services are also made here. The bakery ovens are available at any time to roast meat or bake bread prepared by the women of the village for their own families and celebrations.

The new olive oil factory in the village is equipped with steam stripping equipment from Switzerland (that well-known olive oil country). The olive oil extraction is operated on a cooperative basis, with each farmer getting the oil extracted from his olives and providing labour to operate the equipment and furnace. This is a 24 hour a day operation at the peak of the season.

The village also boasts a pharmacy, part-time clinic, barber shop, dry cleaners, seven general stores, four butchers, the village cooperative office and a small shop which sells plastic flower arrangements and seems to be seasonal.

The name Asites is believed to derive from the original settlers who are said to have come from Assos in Asia Minor. It dates from the days of the Turkish occupation, when few of the inhabitants in the early village were Greeks. The village is located some 20 km due south of the capital, Heraklion, and is just about in the middle of the island when measured both East/West and North/South. It lies about 500 m above sea level, on the side of Koudouni mountain, one of the foothills of Psiloritis, Crete's highest mountain. Before electricity was common in Crete the village men used to climb the mountain daily to cut ice for the hospital in Heraklion. It led to the nickname for Kato Asitans, which has stuck to this day, "Shonades", or snow people. Had we known this earlier, we'd never be here today.

The main road to the south coast from Heraklion used to run through the village but has been superseded by the busy new highway which runs along the bottom of the next valley. This has meant that the towns and villages on this old road have become reasonably tranquil again and are not subject to the mixed blessing of the hordes of traffic that passes along the new road. In stark contrast to the sophistication for which Crete was famous in Homer's day, many villages are now anachronistic backwaters where life has changed little in the millennia since the Minoans were vanquished and Kato Asites, being a mountain village far from the coastal resorts, is a good example.

Our nearest neighbouring village, Ano Asites (Upper Asites), has similar facilities but also boasts a honey bottling plant and a cheese factory. The factory is run by a family who also have a shop in Heraklion to sell their produce. They make cheese from goats and sheep milk provided by people in the village, taking 6 kilos of milk to make 1 kilo of cheese. The process begins by separating the curds from the whey in a heated stainless steel vessel. Heating is by fuel made from the waste products of olive oil production. The curds are scooped out of the vats, wrapped in cheese cloth and dropped into wicker molds. After a few minutes the cheesemaker removes the cheese cloth and drains the cheeses overnight in their baskets. They are then put into storage to mature for at least a month.

They also make sheep's milk yoghurt and mezithra, fresh cheese.

Life in the villages is dictated by the seasons. The day begins at dawn, 5:30 at the end of June and 8:30 at the end of December. Unlike Canada, the gregarious farmers here live in villages and travel to their fields to work; they do not build isolated farmhouses in the centre of their land. Every fine morning starts to the accompaniment of our neighbour's donkey clop clopping down the dawn-lit lane as he sets out for his fields, while across the lane the shepherd roars off on his motorbike up to the mountain pastures. As the day begins to heat up old widows, achromatic in unrelieved black, trek slowly homeward after tending their garden plot, or buying the (literally) daily bread. By 3:30 on torpid summer afternoons the village is asleep and the only sounds are the humming of cicadas and the occasional braying donkey and barking dog.

At the centre of village life everywhere in Crete are the all-male cafenia, coffee shops, gathering places and gossip centres. Michalis the Neighbour claims that the cafenion is the best school for teaching young people (he means young men!) morals and appropriate social behaviour. There are five cafenia in Kato Asites, all scattered along the main street. Each adult male must make the difficult choice when he comes of age of selecting his cafenion. This choice is made according to political affiliation, close friends, previous generations of his family and convenience and proximity to home. Having selected, he then spends the rest of his life visiting it every day. The exceptions to this rule are the village politicians. They can be identified by their impartial patronage of all the cafenia, visiting each of them in turn, to catch the mood of the people, to deliver and receive news and to canvas support for the next election. Among the cafenion hoppers in our village are, naturally, the village president and Giorgos the Post, who although secure in a "tenured" position, likes to keep tabs on the whole village.

Although cafenia are mostly open all day and sometimes long into the night, there are cafenion "hours", when a man can saunter down secure in the knowledge that he will find company with whom to chat, play cards, or simply to sit. During the early morning every able-bodied man is in the fields and the cafenia are empty. When the heat becomes too intense, the cafenia fill with men who step in smartly after a wash and tidy up. On winter days 9 to 11 am is popular. By 1 or 2 pm the cafenia clear as all the patrons are at home being served lunch by their dutiful women folk.

They fill up gradually again after siesta hour, clear out again for the supper hour and are busiest until bedtime. Our neighbour cannot be persuaded to take coffee with us at home during these times, lest he miss an important titbit of village information. Or perhaps our Greek coffee, made in the approved way in the small pot on a gas burner, is still not up to standard.

The etiquette is strict. In the winter men line up against the walls, on warm summer days they sit outside facing the street. It is considered rude to turn your back on fellow customers and there is often a soft shuffling of chairs as a newcomer takes his place. It reminds us of the swifts who roost on the telephone wires near our house. They make a similar movement of wagging tails and ruffling feathers as each new arrival lands on the perch, crowding in line together and chattering greetings.

A coffee is ordered, "eleniko", the strong Greek coffee. Occasionally soft drinks are taken instead and orange is far and away the most popular. Cretans are connoisseurs of soft drinks. Almost every village with a pure spring has its' own factory and each asserts the superiority of the water from which their soft drinks are made. It was several years before we discovered that our village has such a facility. Lefteris the Pop makes soft drinks and distributes them in any available bottles. This means that when you buy this product in the cafenion the legend on the bottle may indicate any of a number of trademarks and places of origin, although it is bottled locally.

There is a mysterious and complicated etiquette too about buying coffee. By a signal we rarely catch the coffee is usually delivered with the compliments of someone sitting at another table. The rules are not entirely well defined, however, and occasionally a good natured dispute breaks out over the privilege of buying an 80 Drachma coffee. We often see Manolis the Taverna make an appearance to buy coffees for all comers in our "local" cafenion, run by Michalis, his nephew. Manolis used to run this cafenion before he built and started operating his taverna. We rarely pass this cafenion without an invitation to join one or more of our friends in a coffee. Often even when we don't take anything to drink we sit and chat with them for a while and pretend we are truly part of this coffee house society.

The only other drink served in the cafenia is raki (the local equivalent of aqua vit or schnapps) and this mostly at night when an impromptu session is started by someone with something to celebrate. These sessions often continue long into the night and all passersby are greeted with jollity and urged to join the party.

In these all male preserves the conversation is mostly agricultural, ranging from the weather and state of the olive or grape crop (depending on the season), to the latest abomination of government policy and the hard life of a farmer. We were in the village for the excitement of the Greek National elections, quite a different proposition from the apathy of the Canadian electorate. We were knee deep in pamphlets and propaganda, with every available wall, billboard and flat surface covered by posters. Enthusiastic public meetings were held almost every night in the village square. There was no shortage of candidates, since every party runs several in each constituency and in Athens, for example, a friend mentioned that she would select up to four candidates of the 19 running for her favourite party. Who gets in depends on the number of votes received in the constituency as well as the success of the party in the country generally. It seems a complicated way to achieve proportional representation. The old gents fossilizing in the cafenion chairs day in and day out in villages across Greece were beside themselves with excitement at having something to talk about.

As Crete is solidly Pasok (socialist), the locals were delighted with the outcome when Papandreou's Pasok party ousted Mitsotakis of the New Democratic Party (which, contrary to its name is the right wing party). This was an interesting comeback for Papandreou since he was kicked out of office several years ago amid a corruption scandal involving millions of dollars, a personal scandal concerning divorcing his wife of decades in order to marry an air stewardess 38 years his junior and several heart attacks leading to doubts about his physical ability to govern at about 75 years of age.

During this election period we discovered that the Greeks have an astute name for politicians, "Kleptocrats", from the Greek word "klepto" (to steal). We also started to wonder about the etymology of the word politician, is it perhaps connected with the word "politai" which means, "for sale"?

No matter which party a farmer supports during elections, it is certain that no one supports any government in power! Complaints about treatment of farmers are rife and the phrase, "they are all the same" rings through the countryside. Strikes are common to protest aspects of government policy and tax evasion is the Greek national sport.

Television has arrived in rural Crete, and the prime time movies were suspended during the election campaign to make way for hours of campaign news and detailed analysis of every candidates' smallest pimples and most trivial thoughts. Many eyes in the cafenion are glued silently to the weather, news or ridiculous soap opera. A typical newscast contained items on an arrest for narcotic drugs, someone murdered with a wooden stake through the heart, a teacher caught giving marks for money and a Turkish boat arrested in Greek waters. Greece has one of its very own nightly soap opera absurdities, called "H LAMPSI", the Brightness. H LAMPSI is notable as being just about the only television programme on Greek TV which starts approximately on time. Schedules in the numerous and popular television magazines may be a week or two out of date and movies regularly start an hour or more late. Why the prime time soap is on schedule is a mystery. Probably there would be national riots if it were late.

When there is nothing on television there is usually enough traffic on the main street to enliven the dull moments. Hawkers trucks drive up to each of the main squares and villagers wander over from the cafenion to see what is on offer. We have seen all manner of seasonal fruit and vegetables, fresh fish, tools, brief cases, kitchen implements, dishes, plastic furniture, clothes, carpets, cafenion chairs, etc., so if you have sufficient patience you don't need to go to Heraklion, eventually whatever you want will come to you.

In Michalis' cafenion we once showed some of the many photographs that we have taken in the village and told the people there that we would gladly provide copies of any that interested them. The photograph in the hand proved to be too great a temptation, compared with the promise of some future copy and a number of them were missing when we recovered the pile. Next time we were more organized and pasted numbered photos on a large board that we fixed to the cafenion wall. Alongside this display we placed a notice in Greek (written by Eugenia) explaining the offer of copies together with a paper to list their requests.

After a slow start we received quite a long list of names wanting one or more of the photographs. Next time we went to Heraklion we had the requested copies made and then had the challenge of identifying the people who wanted them.

Some we knew, some were easy since there was only one person in the photograph, some people started asking for their copies as soon as they had filled in their names, and the rest we asked Eugenia and her family to identify to us. Having identified them we then played the sort of catch games usually associated with Giorgos and our mail. We went to the cafenion at all sorts of times to try to catch our quarry, with limited success. In the end we took the last few sets in named envelopes and gave them to Michalis the Cafenion to distribute.

One old chap came to our house and asked for his photograph. This was odd since we'd given him a copy prior to setting up the display. We brought out the list and asked him to point out his name. After a few minutes searching he admitted it wasn't there. He asked to see the photo display board. He was puzzled not to find his photo there either, we had removed it when we had started to dismantle the display. In the end we concluded that it wasn't worth giving him a hard time for the sake of having an extra copy made and gave him our master of the same photograph that we'd given him previously. He went away delighted after trying once again to pay us for it. Subsequently the man, Yannis, became one of our frequent visitors and we came to know him well. He is 84 years old and a widower of 8 years. Lonely and dissatisfied with his single status, he is famous in the village for his yearning attempts to find a new wife. Perhaps the extra photo was for placing in the personal want ads?

A week later, whilst walking back from Sarhos a distant village down the valley, a man stopped Mike and asked him to sit and eat an orange. This sort of friendly behaviour is not uncommon but this man had a motive other than hospitality. He turned out to be Andreas, one of the names on the photographic list that we did not know. He had received his requested photographs from Michalis and wanted to thank us in person.

In addition to the five men's cafenia there are other facilities for the younger generation. These are called cafeteria and what these three places have in common (besides the fact the every one is run by a Nikos) is that, although the majority of trade is coffee and soft drinks, they all have more or less well stocked bars. They are decidedly noisier and can be located by the ear shattering arrivals and departures of motorcycles or Dad's agricultural vehicle. The oldest of these establishments for boys is the pizzeria on the edge of town. We frequented it in our early days in the village, seduced by the mistaken idea that at a pizzeria we might be able to obtain nourishment, perhaps even a pizza. Other than a few peanuts with alcoholic drinks however, food is not served.

Our village also now has a new "fast food" cafeteria, set up in competition with Manolis' taverna. Souvlaki, chips, "bifteki" (roughly approximating to hamburger) and shrimps are served, straight from the frozen packet into the deep fryer. We had an entertaining time here one night shortly after it opened. It was still suffering growing pains. Since men run tavernas and women run the homes, the brothers who own the place could only be described charitably as embryonic chefs. The chips had to be sent back to be fully cooked. Being totally inexperienced the boys were profuse in their apologies and wanted to throw them out. Having visions of a second batch also still frozen in the centre, we insisted they were redeemable with a few more minutes in the pan. Thus we had our first Greek chips twice cooked in the Belgian fashion (no mayonnaise). Our Athenian guests that evening were hard pressed not to spit out their first taste of the local red grog and sent it back for bottles of retsina.

We cautiously waited for several months of on-site training before we risked another meal in this cafeteria. It had improved greatly but has not subsequently been an unqualified or even qualified success as an eating establishment. However, we have found it excellent for a quiet pre-dinner drink before going to Manolis' taverna.

The third cafeteria is clearly Kato Asites' IN spot. Its young owner is popular and the place is crowded inside in winter and outside on the patio in summer. The latest edition of the sports paper is always left casually on one of the tables. A card table takes centre spot in the middle of the floor, the television is always on, the station being democratically decided by the patrons. It competes with the stereo blasting Cretan pop music from two wall-mounted speakers. Nikos' young son often provides the floor show and, surprisingly, is affectionately welcomed and coddled by the young bloods.

For the very youngest of cafenion-goers-in-training there is an ultra modern video games centre on the high street right across from Michalis' cafenion, where the adults can keep an eye on the youngsters.

For a full blown barbecue meal and excellent company, however, the place to go is still the taverna. An evening visit we made one day after 24 hours of thunderstorms and rain gives a good idea of their hospitality. We arrived at the taverna at 7.30 with soaking wet feet from the street rivers, the only customers. Just as we were sorting ourselves out a mighty flash of lightning caused a terrific bang nearby and all the lights went out. Maria lit a candle while Manolis dashed to phone upstairs to see if the kids were ok. Then he locked up the taverna and we went upstairs to their home.

We thought we'd visit for a few minutes and then leave but they insisted on feeding us whatever they could provide without the electric stove. Maria's home-made "lukaniko" (smoked sausage) was wrapped in foil and put into the fire to heat. It was much better than the sausages we'd bought in a store in town. She made cabbage salad and Manolis went downstairs for bread, wine, lemons and our umbrellas. Manolis brought out some goat cheese made in Ano Asites and then Maria put on a pot of water to make macaroni sprinkled with cheese on top. A feast! Manolis kept on apologizing (most unnecessarily) for the poor food but, as he said, the company was good.

On another occasion when Paula was away Mike went to the taverna alone. Manolis was watching TV with a cup of coffee, waiting for customers. Desultory chat about the news items followed until Maria arrived to make the salad and chips. When the food was ready Manolis brought an extra glass and a small plate containing a tiny piece of pork chop and sat down at Mike's table. He explained that although he had already eaten he was taking this token meal to provide Mike with company. He stayed there drinking and chatting until other customers came in, a table of three followed by one of five, a busy night. Between serving the others he returned to

Mike's table and invited him to a meal at their house since it was inconceivable that a man alone could be cooking meals for himself, despite protests to the contrary. In the end lunch for a couple of days later was agreed. When the bill was requested Manolis refused to give it to Mike, since they had dined together it was not a commercial transaction. A more than usually unseemly scuffle took place with Mike winning and forcing Manolis to accept his estimate of the cost. Confirmation of the lunch date smoothed things over and Mike went home to bed, full as usual.

The family lunch was delicious: "dolmades" (stuffed vine leaves), "gemista" (stuffed vegetables) and fried potatoes, with wine and followed by coffee and spoon sweet, "glyko". Since there had been a national one day strike against the new tax system the vegetable wholesalers in Heraklion were closed. Maria apologized profusely that she was unable to offer the usual salad.

During this period when Mike was alone in Kato Asites returning from a walk he came through Ano Asites just a week before Easter. There was a man mixing cement in the street and Mike greeted him with the usual, formal "Ya Sas". He stopped his work and asked Mike a whole stream of questions, why are you walking alone?, don't you have a car?, where are you from?, etc. Explaining that we live in Kato Asites prompted the question "Why Kato, Ano is much better and we have empty houses?" this question was closely followed by, " How old are you?" When this was answered he said "the same age as me", although he looked much older with his uncharacteristically white hair and moustache.

This coincidence brought on a feeling of comradeship and

hands were shaken. He showed Mike his garden and a pen full of sheep and lambs and suggested that Mike come back in a few days for an Easter lamb. In all the conversation probably lasted for some 15 minutes or more, all in Greek. Mike was quite pleased with himself, although it was apparent that his new friend was making quite large and generous allowance for the many mistakes.

Mike's solitary state was also the cue for our neighbours Michalis and Katerina to provide regular meals and company. On a typical occasion Michalis came bearing a plate of the wild greens that they had cooked for their lunch and waited while Mike ate it with bread as instructed. Michalis identified the little blue flowers, that he had picked but not been able to identify in our flower books, as "stravoksylo". The name comes from "stravos" meaning crooked, twisted, and "ksylo", meaning wood, describing the plants twisting, wandering stems. The word stravoksylo is also used as a term of abuse meaning an obstinate or contrary person. Describing Turks was Michalis' example.

He talked of the times when people from the village used to go up to Koudouni mountain every day for ice. In those days there was a good path from the village to the mountain. It is overgrown now but he still knows it and promised to show us the route. He also repeated his warning about the dangers of climbing in the mountains alone with an additional new twist. He warned that if Mike was seen on his own, by people who didn't know him, there was a good chance that he would be forcibly hauled off to the police in Heraklion as a suspected sheep thief.

Mike mentioned that he intended to catch the first bus on

Saturday to Heraklion to get some tile cement. Early Saturday morning an unknown Greek lady rang. Mike assumed it was the usual wrong number but it was obvious later that it had been Katerina. A few seconds later the phone rang again, it was Michalis offering their son, Manoussos' services to take Mike into town to get the cement. About half an hour later Michalis came over with a bowl of rice pudding covered with cinnamon and said "eat this and then we'll go". While waiting to leave Mike thanked Katerina for all the meals she had sent over and tried, nicely, to ask her not to continue this very generous practice, which must be a strain on their resources.

Having bought the tile cement Mike had planned to leave the Manusakis family and wait more than three hours for the next bus back to Kato Asites. Instead, he was invited to join them and accepted so he could observe their normal Saturday routine. A Palm Sunday procession (on Saturday?) passed, consisting of a collection of girls and women singing while following two palm fronds. The rear was brought up by the priest.

The Saturday market at the port was absolutely packed with a mixture of locals and tourists. Apparently the prices go up in the summer when the tourists are around, but drop just before the market closes at midday. After stops at a watch repairer and a frozen food store they finished at Continent, the new French super-store near Gazi. It was absolutely crazy with the pre-Easter frenzy and although Manoussos and Katerina had been there a few days before they still managed to buy 8 bags of groceries.

That same evening Mike went to the taverna. En route there was a bigger than usual crowd in Kostas' shop. On their already crowded counter they had placed a new machine to grind coffee beans on demand. All the locals were passing judgement on it, as well as stocking up ready for the end of Lent. Unfortunately, the taverna was closed for the last week of Lent during which people observe the fast more strictly. Mike was turning around to go back home when Manolis came up the street on his way to Kostas' shop. He insisted Mike go up to the house for a visit with the family. After talking about English lessons for a few minutes he spent an hour on Greek with Eugenia. It was a domestic evening around the kitchen table writing out irregular verbs while everybody else watched TV.

One of greatest difficulties in the village has been that of obtaining our mail. Many villagers never receive any letters, but since we are still running a business and subscribe to a number of weekly and monthly journals we receive considerably more mail than the average village resident. The postal system should include home delivery but Giorgos the Post delivers only to the shops on the main street and perhaps a few convenient houses. Other people must collect their mail from him. In principle this didn't seem too difficult but in practice we could never find him.

Several times each week we would troop down to the village community office with its one room post office. More often than not, Giorgos, who is supposed to work from 8 to 2 pm, would not be there. Occasionally, perhaps one time in four, we caught him. Upon seeing us, he would begin to root among the pile of untidy bits of paper, mail, discarded envelopes and money (people also pay their electricity and phone bills and receive pensions) and accumulate a small hill of letters, magazines and scientific journals that represent our contact with the outside world. These he would hand over casually, leaving us to wonder if perhaps our missing issues of the New Scientist or Materials Performance are still lurking among the debris.

One day rumours circulated that Giorgos was retiring and we would have a new postman. The rumoured new postman was none other than Giorgos' son, who had just finished a hairdressing course in Heraklion. The rumours suggested that he delivered letters to your very house on the same day he picked them up, even if there were only one! Eugenia marvelled that on two consecutive days around that time she received one card on each day. We went through a phase of leaving our outside gate open all day in the faint hope that we might get some mail delivered to us. However, Giorgos' son soon found greener pastures elsewhere and we were once again stuck with Giorgos' cavalier attitude to the sacred duty of postal delivery.

Some time later Giorgos was evicted from the village office, apparently for spending too much of his time on other activities. He set up his new base in the language school building at the other end of the village near the bakery. This was even more inconvenient since we couldn't now pop down the few steps to the village office to check whether or not he was there. After a couple of weeks of frustration we cornered him in his house and said, "this isn't working, what can we do about it?" Amazingly, he came up with the only possibility that we had thought of, to leave our mail at one of the shops or cafenia. We decided on Michalis' cafenion as being the most convenient and when we approached Michalis he had no objection. Since then we get mail on most days that Giorgos goes to Agios Mironas to collect it. We still have to catch him in his new office to pay our phone and electricity bills but it's certainly an improvement.

Mail delivery is eccentric everywhere in Crete, it seems. We were once nearly run down in the main street of Heraklion by a man weaving precariously slowly on a large motorbike among the pedestrians on the pavement. We watched him in astonishment, since he made no attempt to get back on the road. He stopped in front of a shop and called in to the shop keeper, undertaking her morning sweeping ritual, handed her a pile of letters, then continued his weaving progress along the pavement to the next store.

CHAPTER SIX

An Evening with Homer

Cretans use the Greek language, or some approximation of it, with a strong accent which, inevitably, we are picking up. This distinctive Cretan accent makes Athenians shudder and dismiss us as country bumpkins, which does not worry us at all. It's much more important to us to communicate with our neighbours and friends than to blend in with the Greeks from the capital.

The Cretan dialect is softer and older than mainland Greek. It uses the sh sound for the letter chi (as in the Scottish loch) and often substitutes ch for k. In addition, there are many words where the Cretan version is completely different from the authorized Greek word, like our loquat tree, which here is called "thespola", instead of the mainland word, "mousmoula". (As a consequence of this confusion, it was a long time before we knew what the tree in our garden was.) Some Cretan words, which have been adopted into Greek, may derive from the original Minoan language. Minoan was kept alive into historical (Roman) times by the Eteocretan (true Cretan) remnants of the early inhabitants who survived Mycenean, Dorian and Roman conquests in small population refuges, especially in the east of the island. It is said that there remain fragments of the Cretan language written in Greek letters - an ironical inversion of the Linear B script of ancient Greek written in Minoan. One common Greek word which may be Minoan is "thalassa", the sea.

Since we are learning mainly from listening to the locals we are progressing slowly and we still get confused by the simplest things. For example, in principle it is simple to greet people in the street. In the morning you say "kali mera (good morning)"; in the evening it is "kali spera (good evening)" at night; when leaving people, "kali nikta (good night)". At any time of the day or night you can use "herete (greeting)" or, "ya sas" plural or formal, "ya sou" singular and informal ("to your health") or simply "ya".

All very clear. However, whenever we walk down the street and greet people (we always make the first move and they always respond) we ALWAYS use a different greeting to the one that they choose. There are some clues that we have gleaned: little old ladies like to use, "herete", young bloods use, "ya"! Everybody else uses something other than the one we choose which is either frustrating, annoying or amusing depending on what sort of day we are having. We have now largely adopted the young bloods approach and usually use, "ya"!

There is also another ritualistic conversation which most people run through.

1st Cretan:
"Kali mera, ti kanete, kala eiste? (Good morning, how are you, are you well?)"
2nd Cretan:
"Kala, eseis? (Well, and you?)"

Unfortunately, both 1st and 2nd Cretan say both these lines simultaneously so that this is not the most effective method of finding out about the other person's health.

The conversation will often continue with phrases like,

"I saw Manolis yesterday."

"Which Manolis?"

"Manolis from the shop, Kostas' son. He was going out with Yannis."

"Which Yannis?"

"Yannis, Michalis' son." Etc., etc.

Clearly the locals are also frequently confused by the shortage of variety in names. We once asked why they don't reply with the surname, for example, Fasolakis Michalis. The reply was that there are very probably several Fasolakis Michalis' in the village as well. Naturally, because if several sons have sons each first cousin will be named after the same grandfather! Official community announcements are broadcast over the village loudspeaker and often include lists of names. In these cases names are announced as Markakis, Manolis tou (of, implying "son of") Michali, come pick up your pension. By the way, all Greek names which end in -akis are apparently of Cretan derivation. It means "son of" and derives from the diminutive. The exception seems to be the people of Anogia, the mountain home of renowned freedom fighters. Here they do not use the -akis ending since they do not consider themselves diminutive in any way! The ending -akis is also used in other, sometimes very peculiar forms, such as, have some "winette" (krasakis), from wine (krasi).

Other village announcements give various types of useful information to the community in general. Most of the time we don't understand much of it, but can often catch the drift. A long list of names is usually some business to do with the farmer's cooperative. Other useful messages are, for example: "Today is the last day to pay your electricity or phone bill." "Parents please visit the primary school on Sunday for a discussion of your child's progress." "A special religious service is being held in another village and the bus leaves at 8 am."

Occasionally we miss something of great importance. On our return from one trip we were filling our 1 000 litre water tank during an announcement we could not catch at all. Several days later we learned that the village secretary was announcing that a sheep had fallen in the reservoir and died. "We aren't sure how long it has been there but do not drink the water for a few days till we get around to chlorinating!" After emptying our tank and stocking up with bottled drinking water we learned that the dead sheep had been a hoax.

Paula bears the brunt of most of the Greek conversation in the village because, although Mike understands as much (or, more accurately, as little) Paula is more deceptive in nodding knowingly and murmuring "yes, yes". This used to trick people into believing that she actually comprehended them. Though dishonest, this ruse is sometimes necessary to avoid ever longer and increasingly complex attempts at explanation. Furthermore, we have discovered in Crete that the English do not have a monopoly on that old ploy of shouting loudly at foreigners in order to make them understand. "Katalaves tora? Do you understand now?" By the third "Katalaves tora?" the volume is enough to make you wince.

One day Paula was caught out by Michalis. She said, "yes" where she clearly should have said, "no".

"She doesn't understand at all!", said Michalis disgustedly to Katerina and Paula's stock plummeted in the village conversational stakes. Because, of course, the purpose of conversation is communication, Michalis was visibly upset at the idea that we could convey a misleading impression of comprehension.

A few days later we were sitting in the taverna with the Manusakis family and Eugenia. Michalis asked Eugenia why Paula claimed to understand when she clearly didn't. Eugenia translated the question.

"Because if I didn't, I'd go deaf". Michalis looked surprised for a moment, then burst out laughing.

"Katalaves tora, Michali?"

Whenever our avli (courtyard) gate is open we have a procession of people passing slowly by, peering in at the house. They are naturally curious to see what marvellous things the foreigners are up to and often wander right into the house for a look round. We do not take offense at this; if we resented being an object of curiosity we should have stayed home, where we would not be conspicuous. Besides, when we want privacy, we simply shut the gate, a signal which is nearly always respected. (Hence, the open gate when we thought there was some slim possibility of having our letters delivered by a passing postman.)

With the gate open our day in the courtyard is a series of

courteous greetings from passersby who catch our eye and often stop to engage in small talk. Unfortunately, whenever we open the gate we also receive the unwelcome gift of the village's rubbish, blown in by the wind. We often pick up bits of plastic wrappers from croissants, crisps and chocolate bars dropped by the local children, all of whom are addicted to junk food if they can beg the few hundred drachmas to get it from Kostas' shop. Garbage, garbage, everywhere. In books on Greece we have read several apologetic accounts by foreigners who excuse the Greeks by saying that all the waste used to be degradable until recent times. Rubbish! And more rubbish.

In fact, the truth is that the Greeks are litterbugs. Everyone litters, children, parents, old folks. They excuse themselves with, "It was not me, it was my hand." Plastic bags, water bottles, discarded stoves, beds, used toilet paper, cigarette butts and packets, ice cream wrappers, even kitchen sinks appear in and around all the villages. There is not an inch of pristine countryside anywhere we have ever been in Crete. Every stream bed, every hillside and cliff is an eyesore, drowning in mounds of discarded waste. Worse, sometimes they even have the temerity to blame the tourists! About once a year we are galvanized into a clean-up operation on the street outside our house, where it collects trapped by the uncleared undergrowth outside our neighbour's shed. Most of the time we are overwhelmed by the depressing, unending mountainous supply of it and try not to see it, even as the locals apparently do not.

The people who come through the gate come in phases but one of our earliest frequent visitors was Michalis the

Neighbour. Indeed, we often opened the gate solely in the hope of seeing him or Katerina, whose company we enjoy tremendously. If he was not in the fields, we would hear his deceptively harsh voice crying "Michali", as he swaggered in to see what Mike was doing. On some occasions he did not want anything in particular, he just came because we had not seen him for several days. One day he brought over a plate of that quintessentially Cretan delicacy, horta, or wild greens. After insisting we eat them hot immediately, he invited us for "coffee" in the evening. Although we had planned a taverna evening, we agreed eagerly, postponing the taverna for another day. We were cooking pizza and doughnuts, so when they were ready we took them across with us.

Almost the first question we were asked was "where is your dictionary?" We had foolishly ventured out without our lifeline. Mike dashed back for it immediately. Even the most stilted conversation was impossible without it in the early days and we used it constantly when we spent an evening across the street. Aphrodite, their daughter, who was home from Athens for an extended Christmas visit, took charge of it, looking up the Greek words; we looked up the English words and it passed back and forth from hand to hand many times during the evening. Mike went back to the house again for our small book of medicinal plants of Greece to see if the wild greens were included. The book was enthusiastically perused by Katerina and Manoussos and even Michalis squinted at it longsightedly for a minute. Michalis has little patience for books, however, and would go to extended and imaginative length to find ways to make us understand the meaning of words and phrases so we would not have to resort to the dictionary. His expressive gestures often divulged his meaning long before we could find the word.

During the course of the evening we mentioned that Mike had written a short story and the revelation began an hilarious attempt to translate it. Mike refused the challenge altogether and it was left to Paula, with a vocabulary of some 50 appropriate words. First we had to establish that Mike had not written a diary or a scientific account of our work. It was a fictional story. This beginning took several minutes to establish.

The main theme was easy as it is about a young man with claustrophobia which is a Greek word. He decides to cure himself by living in a dry well, which was difficult, since the dictionary included curable, but not the verb to cure. Paula didn't get very far, anyway, because Michalis immediately interrupted with a demand for an explanation of claustrophobia. We wisely left it to the family to attempt, and a long discussion ensued about fears, of the dark, of crowds, of heights.

Mysterious knockings at the door and faces at the window were evoked. Ghosts were mentioned and Aphrodite pointed up the chimney of the fireplace, indicating that is where they come from. As Paula was sitting next to the fire (she is always closest, as she is always cold and Mike is always hot, and sits furthest away) she looked up the chimney and shouted "Ella, Ella" (come in). Manoussos and Aphrodite almost fell off their chairs laughing, a reaction out of all proportion to the feeble joke. They are, however, always courteous that way.

Michalis could not leave the subject of fears and explained

seriously that many men in the village, "even big men, with moustaches" are afraid of the dark. Imagine that, even men with moustaches! It is a sickness, he said, they are ill. Mike interpreted this to mean that he thought that we should not be slighting them or poking fun, but Paula was not so sure, since Michalis is the first to tease anyone.

Every one of our hesitant sentences of the story was interrupted, for a translation for the others into real Greek, by whoever caught on first. A digression invariably followed. Michalis wanted to know the age of the main characters, which is not mentioned in the story, so Mike had to make it up on the spot. This was easy, since they are very real to him. Michalis also told of the years of his youth, spending days and nights alone on the mountain, a shepherd tending his father's flock and how he would notice the strange behaviour of sheep and dogs before an earthquake. Apparently, the sheep huddle together and bleat, while the dogs start howling just a minute or so before the earthquake is detectible to humans.

The long evening passed in tales and laughter and we went home reluctantly when Michalis began to fall asleep in his chair. Storytelling in ancient Crete must have been thus, with friends and family sitting around the fire during the long winter nights. Winter is, as Michalis says, a time for company. It is easy to imagine a (more competent) storyteller spinning his yarn to the questions, comments and digressions of the assembly.

When we left for home, Paula finished her reading of the Rouse translation of Homer's Odyssey and it was suddenly brought alive. W.H.D. Rouse's 1937 translation is an attempt to write, in modern English, the kind of natural and folksy language Homer used in his day. Many contemporary colloquial and country expressions are used by Homer, there is nothing of the stilted, formal, poetic style favoured by most translators, says Rouse. Reading this account evoked the ancient evenings, with wine, good food and lively, intelligent (if often illiterate) company.

The kind of ancient evening we had just had.

We have had many such evenings with these neighbours, often accompanied by some of our foreign visitors. We always try to take new guests over to meet them because Cretans love to meet new people and hear their tales. For the foreigners there can be no better introduction to life in the Cretan villages.

One of our guests, Dave from Bristol, came with us on another evening at their house. The usual affair, it started with a small amount of food and drink and ended up with a groaning table and more still to come when we finally escaped. Dave was in for a treat because Michalis had been up the mountain on a snail hunt.

Now snail hunting is a tradition in the villages and obeys rigid rules. The best time to collect them is when there has been a rain following several days of sunny weather. The snails are then, as they say in Greek, peripatetic. Or in Australian, they go walkabout. If the weather has been less cooperative and many days of rain have elapsed they can be collected with a light at night, when they are feeding. They are taken live in a bucket but may not be eaten immediately. They are kept for a couple of weeks and fed on flour or macaroni in order to clean their insides. We have been told that in some seasons, particularly in the dry, late summer, this precaution is unnecessary.

Michalis' snails were long time residents and ready for eating. There was a moment of consternation when Michalis came in to say they had disappeared! Manoussos went out with him and eventually they were tracked down. They had climbed out of the bucket and wandered off. Katerina boiled and then fried them in olive oil and served them hot with a modified fork. Michalis demonstrated. One tine was bent in toward the front. We solemnly took up our forks and bent a tine. Then he picked up a snail in his left hand, knocked the apex of the shell sharply with the fork and turned it with the opening facing him. A quick flick of the bent tine in his right hand and the snail was out of the shell, dangling on the end of the fork. We blinked. We all picked up a snail, tapped it timidly and turned it. Flick, Prong and Display. Dave looked slightly surprised at the grey dangling snail at the end of his fork. First time successful. Michalis was ecstatic and lavish in laughing his praise for Dave, who went up several notches in his estimation. Good chap, Dave. Mike also quickly got the hang of it, but, not liking snails very much, he was circumspect about demonstrating his skill.

For Paula this exercise was imbued with particular significance, since her academic speciality is Malacology, the study of molluscs (clams, mussels, octopus - and snails). With extensive theoretical knowledge, she could have told the company (but refrained) that the reason they tapped the end of the shell was to loosen the attachment of the muscle to the apex. (For the same reason, almost all conch shells sold in the Caribbean have a hole in the top where a chisel has been driven through it. Most of these animals have been eaten before the shell is sold. They are tasty and it saves more time than rotting out the animal).

Our previous culinary experience with snails, however, had been limited to French restaurants, where the animals are served in small depressions on a metal snail plate. Occasionally they may be served in the shells, but the naked, canned molluscs are cooked in butter and garlic and restuffed into shells which the living animals would never have recognized as home. The shells are really tiny dishes that are washed and reused each time.

Furthermore, Paula is left-handed and Michalis' flamboyant demonstration had to be twisted backward for her sinister brain. After several embarrassing failures, to the loud derision of the company, she gave up and decided to relearn the technique backwards (i.e. right-handed). By the time she got it right no one noticed but by then she had resolved to quietly drop any comparisons she might have made between teaching malacologists to extract snails and egg-sucking grandmothers.

The highlight of the feast was the sheep's heads, served to the men only, to whom the heavily salted brains were a great delicacy. Mike tried to pass off some of the rich mixture to Paula but with uncharacteristic demureness she insisted the honours go to the more important men. As we left Dave was presented with one of Michalis' "komboloi" (worry beads) as a gift, in recognition of his snailing talents and for being an all round good chap.

One of the boldest visitors among our neighbours is a small girl named Lefteria, Ritsa for short. Her large family lives across the lane from us and her puckish face was one of the first we ever saw peering around our gate during the first timid days when we dared leave it open. She had obviously just begun English lessons because the first word she spoke to us, with her cheery smile, was "Goodbye". Mostly, however, she just quietly stared. In the early days she became a regular, if infrequent visitor at the gate whenever something particularly eventful was happening at our house during her after school hours. The arrival of our goods prompted a brave incursion right into the house and we showed her the whole of the inside. Shortly after this her mother began to greet us in a friendly manner, so the visit was certainly reported.

Another familiar face at the gate is old Yannis the Widower who passes a dozen times a day, always with a friendly greeting. During the spring season he brought some artichokes and offered some of his cherries, straight from the tree in his allotment.

"Cherries", he said several times, to ensure we understood. "From my allotment. Cherries. It is very near, the allotment. Cherries, do you understand?"

We waited all the next morning but must have had a mix up in communication, with him waiting at his house, us at ours. After a day or so more of confusion, we finally managed a rendez-vous, as again he poked his head around our garden gate. We dressed for walking while he closed up his house.

We trooped after him through the village lanes like ducklings after a mother duck clad in black shirt and pants and the traditional Cretan knee-high black leather boots. Yannis walked with small steps, slowly and carefully; he has a severe cataract in one eye and doesn't see well. Apparently he has been told by the doctor that they can do nothing about it. He greeted everyone he passed as we followed him. Some of the younger, stronger men were a little patronising toward him, not recognizing themselves in forty years.

The lanes led to a footpath on the outskirts of the village and still we trooped quietly on, over two small streams which will dry up in the heat of the high summer, already they smelled a little high. People were trickling back to the fields after the afternoon siesta. One was cutting oats by hand for winter fodder. He was standing amidst neat bales, the uncut crop towered up to his shoulder. We circled round till we were almost in the village again and at a house on the outskirts Yannis stopped and called to the owner while a vicious dog barked furiously. Yannis' nephew came out and held the snapping, snarling, barking dog by the chain while we scuttled timorously past, one by one. Behind the dog was a padlocked fence around Yannis' garden. The lock was wholly superfluous. Nothing would induce a sane thief to trespass near that frustrated and starving looking beast for the mere temptation of a few vegetables.

The cherry trees were laden with black ripe fruit and Yannis made a gesture at once dismissive and seigniorial. "Pick away." We picked. Fingers and mouths red with juice we picked in serious silence, one for the bag and one for the mouth. Soon we had picked several kilos but with Cretan generosity Yannis would not let us stop picking until we protested several times.

Yannis was very proud of his large productive plot, with its cherry, loquat, peach, apricot and olive trees as well as grapes tomatoes, onions and other seasonal crops. He has, however, given part of it to his niece and nephew because they had no garden.

We skirted gingerly past the dog which seemed inadequately restrained and were too afraid to pass him again to accept an offer of loquats. Yannis stayed with his relatives and we strolled slowly home with our delicious crop.

CHAPTER SEVEN

Rats and Winter Fuel

SEVEN

One of the more annoying aspects of our work on the house has been our ongoing battle with rodents. Rats have been a recurring theme, they have been with us right from the very beginning when we distinguished this house from the others we were shown as the one-with-the-dead-rat-in-the-back-room. We have been engaged in a desperate battle to evict them from our well-ventilated premises. Many were the nights we sneaked downstairs with a torch to startle them into revealing their access points. Many were the following days that we toured the rooms with ladder, torch, concrete and filler foam, sealing up any likely point of entry. By midsummer, it appeared that our strategy (Greek word) was working and we had achieved a rat-free environment.

Coriander and napkins provided the clues. Elementary my dear Watson. The top right hand drawer contained the napkins and place mats and was rather full. We pulled out the drawer but the napkins which had been neatly folded, stuck. Assuming the napkins had caught on the top as sometimes happens with full drawers, we extracted them for refolding. The napkins, however, were tangled into a nest, virtually every one ripped by nasty little rat teeth dragging it into place.

The top left hand drawer contained the spices. When this one was opened, it was immediately clear that the rat's favourite spice is coriander. Among the wide variety of whole, ground and mixed herbs and spices the rat had rejected almost all others. Only the coriander bags had been chewed open and tasted; curry powders were unscathed; cloves were not required for toothache. The coriander seeds were a mess of plastic bits, rat poop and husks.

The cupboard below the sink was also apparently a nice place to be, for potatoes and onions were available for dining, but only once the furniture was rearranged.

We examined the counters carefully. These were the assemble-yourself kitchen set that we had brought from Canada and had discovered a curious thing as we put them together. Each unit of drawers or cupboards is a separate cabinet. The cabinets then screw together in any combination to fit any kitchen plan. In this model, however, the drawers do not extend the full length of the cabinet and the drawer boxes do not extend to the full height of the drawer face. Thus, having gained entry into a cabinet, the rat is free to wander between floors like in a multi-storey hotel. The substantial gap between the cabinets and the worktop makes access trivial. The whole kitchen set, in fact, was probably designed as a kind of rat-cote by a malicious, rat-faced little man with peculiar hobbies.

Furthermore, there was no back at all on the cabinet under the sink (as is often the case to make room for all the water and drainage pipes). So as long as the rat could get behind the cabinets, there was no impediment to dallying in the cupboard under the sink. And because of the undulating walls (and floors and ceilings) the counter top touches in a few places at the backsplash but the cupboards are several centimetres away at the floor.

By moving the sink and nailing a board up the edge, we could block up the one side of the sink. The other side, however, had been covered by a seat and box combination meticulously designed by us to cover the water pipes. Thus to block that other side would now mean disassembling the entire structure. We could only hope that the rat took the easy route and hadn't discovered the secret passage. We put down some coriander seeds to tell if he paid another visit and went to bed.

War was declared. For the next three nights we maintained a vigil, listening to scurryings and gnawings, searching for clues to his whereabouts. A few minutes sleep was snatched between whispers of "There! Hear that? Do you think that sounds like the spice drawer or under the sink?"

About 3 am on the third night Paula woke up to find a naked Mike rooting around among the suitcases and boxes in the bedroom, muttering to himself.

"I know you are here you bastard, come out." After a few moments, when she was thoroughly awake, Mike went downstairs again, to gaze at the rafters in the hope of finding his lair. Seconds later the rat made a dash for it across the bedroom floor and Paula calmly alerted Mike to the fact that he was nearly in bed with her. "Heading toward the stairs" was no sooner out than there was a scramble at the bottom and Mike emitted a peculiar cry that can only be described as an orgasm of frustration.

"If only I'd had a slipper in my hand I'd have got him." Mike resolved to remove one slipper at the bottom of the stairs and one slipper at the top when he retired to bed in future.

The next, exhausted morning we had come to a unanimous decision. No more mister nice guy. We looked up mousetrap in the dictionary and trooped in tandem (we always went out together, for mutual support in unknown territory) to the village hardware store. They were in stock. We bought two. The owner also offered to sell us some "deleterio" (poison) but we decided against it on the ground that you never know where the buggers go to die. Then we went outside to look for more potential entry holes, this time in the outside walls. We now believed that these creatures were capable of traversing kilometres inside solid stone walls, possibly entering via our less vigilant neighbours' houses. During this examination we found a hole the size of a small child behind our own electricity box, which was directly outside the kitchen area where we had heard most activity. We grimly dropped pebbles in and covered the lot with cement.

While we were thus engaged several neighbours passed by and asked were we stopping leaks, as the rainy season had just started. "No. Mice", we said with Victorian delicacy for euphemism. Also, having looked up the word for mousetrap, we now knew the word for it. To a wo/man, they evoked the magic word, deleterio.

Our neighbour, Michalis, elaborated. "They are too smart for traps. I have some poison."

In fact, it became clear that the entire village is intimately familiar with the methods of rat eradication.

We were in bed only twenty minutes when the trap snapped, followed by a muffled squeaking and flapping about.

"Eeuuugh, you go."

"No you go."

"Let's go together."

The first trap in the bathroom was still intact. We approached the cupboard door under the sink with trepidation. Opening it partway we both screamed and slammed it shut again as the flapping resumed. We were both horrified at having caught the poor thing, which naturally now looked small, pathetic and victimized. We dropped the rat, trap and all into a bucket of water to minimize the suffering of the pitiful creature that Mike would so happily have squashed bare handed the night before. We put the bucket outside, to deal with it in the morning when we were stronger and when the rat would surely be dead. Fortunately the next day was garbage collection day. Did you put the rat out?

In the meantime, we had been so successful in preventing ingress of cats into the shed, that there was now mounting evidence that we had traded them for a rat problem there too. We set the trap again, baited with the same cheese and the next morning the trap was sprung, cheese was gone and the rat had defecated all around it in a lovely pattern of thanks-for-dinner. Mike attributed the getaway to luck but Paula grasped instantly that it must have come from the neighbour's, where they have cleverer rats. We were dealing here with a fiendishly skilful trap evader. It's time to outsmart a rat. For several nights, we would bait the trap with cheese but not set it. When the rat was lulled into complacency we would set the spring and zap.

We were so impressed with the superiority of our intelligence over rat-dom that we put the plan into action at once, not waiting till dark. By night the cheese was still there, but this was not conclusive defeat because rats are nocturnal. The cheese was still there the next morning. And the next. And the next. With two PhD's between us we couldn't outwit a single rat.

After that episode we were engaged in a running battle with rats in the shed. Each night we set two traps and eventually achieved a pretty high success rate, both traps loaded on a good night. Rather than continue this for the rest of our days we had also been making strenuous efforts to seal the wall between us and the livestock and feed storage building next door. Victory was an uphill struggle since the walls are riddled with rat highways and they can usually find a weak spot to break out of when we seal their usual exits. At least the locals assertion that rats were too smart to be trapped seems to have been well disproved.

It was a proud moment when we decided we had progressed far enough with the construction work to begin purchasing household items. By lucky coincidence, our refrigerator purchase coincided with the establishment of a new electrical shop in the village. Zacharis the Electric has a shop in Heraklion and decided to branch out into the village. He comes from Kato Asites and his parents still live here. With a small shed full of wire and light switches in the ancestral home and another room full of more enticing electrical items and, of course, with a built-in labour force (when Mum and Dad are not in the fields), all that remained was to erect a sign advertising his wares. His arrival was providential for us. It meant that we could buy our fridge without worrying about delivery. Zac came out from Heraklion by appointment and we picked up, almost incidentally, several metres of electrical cable, some switches and wall outlets and then began on the fridge.

It was soon clear that the issue wasn't as simple as fridge/freezer. For one thing, we wanted the door to open to the left, which isn't standard. When it became obvious that we needed more information than his brochures could give, we agreed that we should meet at Zac's Heraklion store where more catalogues, specifications and facilities were available. And then we had a very strange lesson in Greek culture.

Zac tried to describe to us the location of his shop. We narrowed it down to a street off one of the main roads into Heraklion, outside the Hania gates. So far, no problem. It was the detailed description which confused us. His entire set of directions depended on our knowing the location of those small kiosks which are called in Greek, "periptero". We had never seen any.

More accurately, we had seen lots of them but we had never NOTICED them. Zac was astonished. The periptero is central to Greek daily life and supplies all the essentials. People stop by several times a day to buy cigarettes, to use the telephone, to buy water or a quick snack. Consequently, everyone knows all the kiosks in town and they are used as landmarks, like pubs in Britain and gas stations in Canada. (When there isn't a periptero there is a church, so Greeks are never at a loss for directions.) It was a major cultural lesson, one we have never forgotten, which is just as well since we have since been given directions many more times in reference to the periptero down the street.

To provide light relief amongst our major construction projects we decided to start digging out the well. This had been used as a rubbish dump for many years, presumably since the town supply of water arrived at the gate. The top of the rubbish was initially some 5 or 6 metres from the top of the well. We checked Michalis the Neighbours' well and found that he has water at about the 25 metre level. Setting up our climbing ropes and harness Mike abseiled down to the top of the pile and Paula lowered down a spade and bucket. The top few items, large metal tubs, plastics sacks and chunks of wood were quickly removed. The next stratum was interspersed with thick layers of ash and contained soft drink cans and bottles, old clothes, thousands of used ampoules of an unknown medication and sacks of household refuse. We dug and sorted and hauled and after several long sessions had reached the 10 metre level. Michalis came over just as we were about to start one of these digging sessions and had a good chuckle at Mike disappearing into the well on the end of a climbing rope.

When our first year's stock of olive wood for the winter stove was just about depleted we began to think seriously about the forthcoming winter months. As our supply had been a most generous and unexpected gift from Michalis, we were at a loss to know how to replenish it. We saw a lot of wood around the village. As winter approaches huge olive trunks are stockpiled around various points outside homes and at the edge of the village. The trunks are removed by dynamite or large mechanical diggers when old trees are replaced by young ones. Each trunk weighs several tonnes and they are split by mechanical splitters which were more familiar to us on city streets where they break up tarmac roads during repairs to sewage and water pipes. Truckload after truckload of this wood is loaded onto the Piraeus ferry for export to Athens, Germany and elsewhere.

These enormous chunks were hardly suitable for our small winter stove. All the families around us have their own olive groves and seem to have a ready supply of wood for winter. Michalis himself has an entire wall of many metres neatly stacked from floor to ceiling, at least two or three years supply. One evening as we sat around Katerina's warm and welcoming stove, we asked the family how to go about buying wood in the village. With characteristic helpfulness Michalis told us that several people in the village sell wood. He recommended his relatives, who would sell us excellent olive branches (roots are considered inferior and are avoided by villagers). He told us how much it costs, that it is sold by weight. Not having even the faintest clue how much volume 1 000 kg of wood occupies, Katerina laughingly told us it is not a houseful or roomful, but approximately a mechani full.

Having ascertained we were still hopelessly ignorant, they then phoned up their relatives and settled the purchase of 1 000 kg the very next day at the advantageous price of 20 Drx/kg. Michalis suggested that if we were happy with the quality, we should buy more, since wood was then plentiful and cheap in the village. We hadn't considered that the supply might fluctuate over years, but of course it makes sense that trees mature and grow old in cohorts.

Michalis threw more excellent baking potatoes into the stove. When they were cooked he pulled them out and smashed them open with his hand. "You should never use a knife", he said. Mike watched him with a gleam in his eye and when the next potato was ready Michalis handed it to Mike to open. Still steaming, the potato was juggled lightly for a minute and then ... SMASH. Bits of potato flew across the room. Michalis thought this was hilarious and thereafter every potato was handed to Mike, who learned a gentler touch. A few minutes later Zacharis the Wood zoomed up on his motorcycle and came bouncing in the door, sidestepping bits of potato. Thus we were introduced to our olive wood supplier and one of the village swells.

Zac was much in demand at the moment for his current dining out story. A few days before, in the dead of night, two houses in the village were raided by the Greek special police. With balaclava covered faces they drew their guns and swept into Zac's house to search for illegal weapons.

"Illegal weapons" is a kind of relative term in Crete, since what with all the wars and rebellions there have always been large numbers of arms of various vintages floating around the mountains. These have been pilfered from bodies, taken in battles, stolen in raids and passed down from father to son. They range from small hand guns to semi-automatic rifles. EVERYONE has at least one, it is an open secret. They are fired off during celebrations and are generally quite harmless, for guns.

Zac's family, being in the olive wood business, also possess dynamite for blasting the enormous stumps out of the ground. All in the line of business, and all used for peaceful purposes (unless you happen to be an olive tree). In any case, the police found all these weapons and with a rough half nelson arrested Zac's father and grandfather from their beds and dragged them off to the police station in Agios Mironas and on to jail. It was on the Kriti TV News the next day and caused a flurry of excitement in the village. The supermarket was packed with people the whole day, newcomers being filled in with all the details as they came through the door. Kostas sat behind the cash register and Aristea presided over the gossip like the chairman of a meeting. Paula spent an hour there herself, having gone down simply for a loaf of bread. It took rather longer to explain the story to her, what with all the unfamiliar vocabulary, like special police, arrest, prison, etc. Everyone talked at once, adding to her confusion and the length of the tale. There are some great mimes in the village, though and occasionally someone came in who had a reputation for knowing English and was pressed into service.

It was generally agreed that someone must have "split" on the family, since otherwise, why pick on their houses especially? Faces were serious when discussing this possibility but it was discretely taken no further and there was no speculation on who might have called down the wrath of the balaclavas on the house. Zac repeated his story to the assembled family around Katerina's stove with the sombre, slightly distracted air of one imparting serious news for the thousandth time. Michalis interrupted frequently to clarify small points and enhance juicy details. The story came even from Zac, however, only second hand. By his own admission, he had slept through the entire drama!

Having finished the tale, he promised to meet us at his wood pile near Agia Triada church the next morning at 9, drank a raki in one gulp and was gone.

It was almost 10 am before we were climbing the hill the next morning but Zac came swooping up behind us and assured us in his rapid and slangy Cretan that his "copela" (pal) Vasilis would meet us at the site to split the wood to our requirements. A few minutes later, they both arrived on the bike bouncing dangerously on the rocky road. No work could start before the ritual coffee and Zac bounced off to procure a bottle of water. Four plastic cups with lids, instant coffee and sugar all individually wrapped and ready for making frappe were passed round. Then a chain saw was procured and for the next three hours wood was lifted, sawn, split and thrown onto a growing mountain. When the chain came loose Zac roared off and returned with his cousin and another saw. In the meantime we had fixed the broken one with Paula's trusty Swiss army knife and Vasilis and Mike continued augmenting the mountain.

Soon there were two saws going in tandem, with a cool one replacing the overheating machine, while Manolis, Zac's baby-faced, attractive young cousin split the blocks which wouldn't fit the stove opening. The heavy axe was clearly too much for him but he gamely split the dense wood. We watched with breath-catching anxiety as the axe landed repeatedly within centimetres of his booted foot. To express our concern would only increase the swagger, so we watched with silent apprehension.

The boys epitomised the macho Cretan youth, flaunting their strength and cavalierly waving and flashing the noisy, phallic chainsaw. They were clearly showing off and checked regularly to see that we were still admiring their skill.

When our attention flagged Vasilis brought out an immense olive branch and attacked it with the saw. The size of it gave us an idea and we had Zac cut off a large slice which, when planed and polished, made a commendable chopping block for our kitchen.

When Vasilis estimated that the mountain was large enough, the boys disappeared again. Vasilis fetched his truck and Zac came chugging up the hill in an enormous earth mover. He scooped up the security lock, a 2 tonne olive trunk which was parked in the entrance to the woodyard, and pushed it out of the way. Vasilis backed his truck in, loaded it to the axles and we drove off to the weigh scales at the olive oil factory. The drive-on scales are available for all comers and we piled out of the truck to balance the weights.

With difficulty, the 700 kg of the empty truck weight was deducted from the total and Zac laboriously recorded 850 kg of wood on a scrap of paper we provided, using the pen from the army knife. This was the third time it had been used this morning and it was surreptitiously admired, the boys not wanting to be overt about liking the possession of a mere female.

After measuring the width of the narrow lane, even the boys were convinced that the truck could never be brought up to the gate. They called for the wheelbarrow and swiftly procured a second one from the neighbours. Within minutes the truck was unloaded and, refusing a rest or a coffee, they dashed off to load up and deliver the remaining wood.

By 3 pm we were the proud owners of 1 350 kgs of winter warmth. The work done, the boys finally condescended to come in for a restorative raki, then another raki, then some wine and a mountain of chips, horta, tomatoes and cheese. Zac was knocking back the wine at a tremendous rate and was animatedly regaling us with stories we couldn't understand but were presumably his exploits. He began to talk about Morocco and it took us some time and considerable miming for him to convey to us that it is the name of a nightclub in Heraklion where women take off their clothes. With enthusiasm Zac conveyed the notion by miming several times the removal of his t-shirt. His interest was so serious and so virginal that Paula began to be suspicious about his age. This being Crete, it is quite permissable to ask such personal questions. Zac was only 15 years old! Furthermore, his "young" cousin, Manolis, is exactly the same age. Their trusty wood spitting companion, Vasilis, is a venerable 30 years old.

Michalis made a fortuitous entrance just as the boys were staggering and sliding away and he pronounced that our wood was indeed good quality. We arranged for the delivery of a second load the following Saturday and Zac came bouncing into the yard Friday morning to confirm the arrangement. A few minutes later we saw his father as we were going out for our stroll. He said that Zac had commented on our prodigious table and laughed at the state the lad had come home in. We were pleased since in Crete hospitality is a vital component of life and we have an enormous reputation to live up to, not to let the "foreign" side down. We sometimes wonder whether our livers will survive all this good will!

On Saturday afternoon, while Vasilis and Zac unloaded two

full truckloads of wood, we busied ourselves with the less arduous task of chopping chips and stacking wine glasses. Although we carefully refrained from asking Zac about the state of his head on Thursday morning he was extremely circumspect the second session, refusing food and drinking only two small glasses of wine. Lest we thought he was unwilling to get involved in another session, he carefully explained that he had "work" in Heraklion. "What kind of work?", we asked, "With women!", was the answer.

A few weeks later we bought another 1 000 kgs of wood from our other neighbour, Yannis, to show impartiality and goodwill. This load completely filled our available storage space.

Shortly after, Michalis the Neighbour called us over to his house. Zac was there eating a sweet, standing alongside his mechani. Michalis, in his usual blunt manner, explained that Zac wanted to go out with his friends, had no money and also had a lot of really good wood. We worked out the implication and said we'd take another load or two, and rationalised it as an investment. We spent an hour clearing additional space to put this extra supply. Our shed by now had little room for anything else.

He promised to come the next day so we removed the shed doors and stayed home waiting for him. He didn't arrive. We had just about forgotten about the wood delivery and were going for an afternoon walk several days later when we heard a mechani being driven somewhat inexpertly and erratically behind us. It was Zac with one of his pals. He caught up with us and asked whether we wanted the wood delivery now. We agreed but asked him to wait for another half an hour, being unwilling to give up our walk completely. They roared off and we walked over to the old mill in the gorge below Ano Asites.

Returning in half an hour or so we only had to wait another half an hour before two mechanis turned up, driven by Zac and his pal, the butcher's son. They unloaded the 2 000 kg of wood while we furiously stacked up to the roof. Just as we finished jamming the last sticks in Zac said he would be getting some REALLY good wood soon, did we want some more? We declined and paid for the current delivery. They left, refusing the food and drink we offered. Perhaps Zac still had memories of a hangover? We now had enough fuel for 5 or 6 winters so another one of our little problems had been solved, and our shed smelled like the olive oil factory it was once.

Just after the boys left our young pal Ritsa came in for a visit. Almost as soon as she arrived there was a faint call outside in the lane and she dashed off to bring in her friend, Elizabeth. Although Ritsa refused an orange drink, she encouraged her friend to accept and after sitting daintily on the edge of a chair while it was being drunk, Ritsa began a voyage of exploration. First she examined our panorama of the village, photographed from the top of our roof. Then she asked whether we had any other photos and we extracted our considerable collection and settled down on the couch with a small, attentive girl on either side. When she came to a picture of a cat sitting on top of their garden wall, Ritsa pressed it ecstatically to her breast, exclaiming, "Oh, our kitty cat" in loving tones. Her exhibition of affection would have been more convincing had we not heard her happily torturing the poor thing frequently enough before it grew wiser and faster.

When bored with the photos Ritsa bossily showed her small friend the library, then the upstairs bedroom. When they spotted our computer they asked whether they might write a word. They are the first villagers ever to dare touch our computer. It was a disappointing instrument for them, since it does not have a Greek keyboard but they were consoled by being able to spell out small words from their English lessons and amused themselves for at least an hour. English versions of the names of brothers and sisters were also entertaining. If Ritsa hit a wrong key and the computer did something unexpected she gasped in chagrin until we assured her that it didn't matter, and undid her mistake.

CHAPTER EIGHT

Celebrations Cretan Style

EIGHT

Our first village celebration was, appropriately, at the taverna, at the invitation of Eugenia and her family. It was being held in honour of farmers who had just returned from a training course in France on phylloxera, the devastating grape disease caused by an infestation of small, deep burrowing, yellow insects. France can claim some expertise on this grape disease since it devastated the French wine industry before the turn of the century and many oenophiles claim that French wine has never been the same since.

The local farmers were being presented with certificates by the federal minister who came from Athens for the celebration and a reporter from Kriti TV was present. We arrived at 7:30, and sat stiffly with all the farmers and their wives, all dressed in their finest. The tables were set with baskets of bread and nothing else. A tardy husband arrived and we moved politely one seat over, making room for him to sit by his wife. He spread his arms in a dramatic gesture and exclaimed to the table, "I have been sitting next to her for 43 years!" He grumbled as he reluctantly took the seat. They spent the entire evening literally with their backs to each other, conversing with their opposite table companions. Another long married couple took more direct action. They had arrived early and were sitting next to one another but as soon as a favourite cousin arrived the wife emphatically rose and forced the young man to squeeze past her and sit between them, isolating her from her husband. Women can't afford to waste any opportunities out of the house to converse with novel companions and husbands are very poor currency at parties.

When the Minister arrived at 9 pm (he was probably invited for 8) everyone sat down. Maria had been sitting quietly composed on a chair in the kitchen doorway, resting her aching legs, waiting for the "word". Now she sprang into action, rising and moving to the kitchen for food preparation. The minister made a short speech in response to a welcome address and everyone brightened and got ready for the food.

First came various whisky bottles. Whisky? No, they were filled with local red wine. The homemade, foot-stomped wine is called red, looks like rosé, tastes like sherry, and kicks like overproof navy rum. Then came small plates heaped with boiled rice and large communal plates of boiled meat of unknown origin, possibly lamb. The flavourful rice was pilafi, a Cretan speciality, cooked in stock, margarine and lemon. We were proud of ourselves for keeping up with the locals by eating all of our rice, although we only ate a little meat.

After everyone had finished Manolis brought out cabbage salad. Ah, we thought, the French style, salad after the meal. When enormous plates were brought out overflowing with huge chunks of roast meat and roast potatoes, we couldn't believe it. "Second plate," said Eugenia blithely. We did our best but we were defeated, having spent all our appetites on the rice. We couldn't keep up. After most of the meat had disappeared large bowls of oranges and apples appeared.

Throughout dinner the local band, all-male of course, played traditional Cretan music, which is wild and unpredictable, quite different to the more western and familiar strains of bouzouki music from the Greek mainland. The main theme is played on the Cretan lyra, the traditional three-stringed instrument made of mulberry wood. It derives from the 7-stringed Minoan lyra pictured on many vases and frescoes. It resembles a violin but is rested on the knee while being played. The accompaniment is provided by the laouto, a kind of lute, and the mandolino. The singer alternates with the lyra to provide the melody. The lyra player stops playing while he sings. This traditional type of music is still very popular in the village even amongst the young people. They have not yet succumbed to the international pop music culture.

The verses are called "mantinades" and are 15 syllable couplets with a lot of humour and spirit, often created spontaneously. The lyrics are mainly on the theme of love, love for Crete, love for a woman. Teenaged Eugenia and her cousin liked these romantic songs and wrote down some of the lyrics. Her cousin had just passed an entrance exam for a two year training course for the hospitality industry, learning languages (German and English) and hotel trades. She was a thoroughly modern miss who told us she intensely disapproved of the traditional female role. Sometimes she got so angry about the restrictions of village life that she went out alone at night just to wander around and make her protest. This doesn't sound very vehement since there is no possible harm she could come to in the village (with the possible exception of being run down by a mad motorcyclist). She risked, however, the ruin of her virginal reputation among the old women and, of course, the men.

Although sheltered, unmarried girls are not actually forcibly confined and the times are changing. During a stroll around the village one day we saw a young village girl and boy, both around 16-18, doing some very energetic necking in broad daylight in the gateway of the nursery school. Still, village celebrations, in which all the family participates, are among the few mixed social occasions sanctioned by the community for unmarried girls.

Cretans have always expressed their feelings and mood in dance, a tradition introduced to the world by the bon-viveur peasant in Kazantzakis' "Zorba the Greek". Zorbas is alive and well and living in all Cretan villages. Anyone who wishes to request a particular dance gives some money to the leader of the musicians and they play the appropriate accompaniment. The person who requested the dance then leads it. Everyone participates - toddlers, teenagers, faltering grandmothers. It is all done in a rough, never closed circle. The leader at the front is changed regularly and many kick out and leap in energetic moves that reflect their feelings.

The Greeks traditionally believed that the oldest dances in the world were Cretan and originated in the exuberant high leaps and wild shouts of the semi-mythical Curetes as they were trying to drown the cries of the Earth Mother's newborn son Zeus, so that he would not be devoured by his jealous father, Chronos. Although the identity of the Curetes is unknown, they may have been a tribe of Cretan people. In Lilian Lawler's fascinating book, "The Dance in Ancient Greece", she notes that dances were associated with religion from the beginning. Leaping dances were performed to quicken the growing forces in nature and ensure fertility as well as to ward off evil spirits.

A surviving fragment from the famous poet from Lesbos, Sappho, says, "Thus once upon a time the Cretan women danced rhythmically with delicate feet around a beautiful altar, treading upon the soft, smooth flowers of the meadow." Circle dances, says Lawler, are of mystical significance to many ancient people and are often performed around an altar, tree, pillar or musician. Minoan vases and sculptures in the Heraklion Museum depict many such scenes. The Minoans probably used them to invoke the Great Goddess.

At this modern farmer's celebration about half a dozen different circle dances were repeated. When the music was very fast the old folks bowed out and the young ones leapt and bounced. One dance was for women only, it was wonderful to watch and hypnotic to participate in. Every region of Crete has its own special dances hence, for example, the Haniotis from Hania. One of the young girls was kind enough to tell us that we danced well, which was so patently untrue that the comment served mainly to emphasise how thoughtful and hospitable they were.

The usual manner in which to express approval of the dancing is to smash plates on the floor in amongst the dancers. The dance proceeds over the debris. Before coming to Crete we had believed this to be a trick of the Greek tourist trade's Traditional Evening. Now we discovered it is very much a living custom, even at private family celebrations. Giorgos, an accomplished dancer, was leading one of the dances, when Manolis went into the kitchen and returned with an armful of dinner plates. He threw them into the air with great gusto and they smashed in the middle of the circle of dancers who responded with shouts and renewed demonstrations of skill. Giorgos detached himself from the circle and began an expressive, intricate, solitary performance while the others went down on one knee and encouraged him by clapping hands in time to the music.

As the normally very temperate farmers drank more of their

class material the pace grew louder and the din more frenetic. In a hot, smoke-filled fug in the closed winter room the group danced and drank and shouted. It is a curious feature of Cretan drinking sessions that the small glasses are never more than one third filled. Since almost every time wine is poured a new toast is called for, drinkers seem to toast with every sip. "Si Yeea, (Health)!" "Stin yia sas (to your health)!" and "Ya mas (Our health)!" eventually give way to the more exuberant, "E Viva!" Lacking the stamina for graduate study we left early but these parties always carry on till 4 or 5 am.

Since this first time we have attended many such celebrations, weddings, baptisms, school fund raisers, etc., and they all seem to follow this pattern. They also all produce the same effects of sore eyes and streaming noses from the smoky atmosphere and headaches from too much of the local wine. A small price to be paid the next day. Paula is an especially enthusiastic, if not very proficient dancer and stumbles her way through the most complicated dances.

In Crete people do not generally celebrate their birthdays, but their saint's name day. As everyone in the village seems to have one of only half a dozen names, these evenings are quite rowdy. Girls, who are named after their grandmothers, don't count and don't celebrate their name days in such spectacular fashion. This is more reasonable than it appears at first because the celebration consists of the women spending all day cooking and serving large quantities of food and booze to a random selection of relatives and friends who show up to wish the celebrant "Cronia polla", roughly equivalent to Happy Birthday or Happy Name Day, literally, "Many Years". This would be just too exhausting if you were both the cook/waitress and celebrant.

Not to mention that after the first four dozen or so wellwishers had joined you in a toast to your health, you would not be in any shape to serve newcomers. It would be unthinkable for the men to help except in serving wine.

Name days, unlike birthdays, are very public and are known to everyone. Throughout Greece, it is considered polite to offer your wishes in person, if possible, to all friends and relatives on their day. These greetings are graciously offered also to other family members, "for your father/wife/child". When the loved one is far from home, the next best thing is the telephone. Consequently, the celebration of name days has unexpected repercussions. On half a dozen days of the year, such as Kostas, Michalis, etc., the exchanges are overloaded and it is as impossible to get through on the phone as it is on Christmas day in England.

Typical of such affairs was the Kostas day party we went to on May 21st of our first year in Kato Asites. This particular Kostas party was held in Kostas' and Aristea's house above their shop. This is our local supermarket and is open from around 8 am to midnight every day of the year, manned during the siesta time (and any other unsociable occasions) by Nikos their 16 year old son.

We were told that this party would start at 9 pm but we thought we now understood the Greek social scene well enough to know that we must not go at that time. Our problem, on the other hand, was to stay up long enough to go to a party so late. We compromised on going at about 9:45 and killed several hours attempting to send a fax to Kostas our Athenian friend saying "Cronia Polla".

Aristea was just going into the shop and saw us coming. We went in with her and enjoyed a scene typical of Christmas - people frantically buying last minute presents for all the Kostas' parties they were going to. One lady, all dressed up, was agonizing over a gaudy glass tray with small flowers set in the bottom, one of several of similar design and different shapes on display in the shop. She finally selected one at 5 450 Drx for which Kostas only took 5 000 Drx. (Crete is the only place we have ever been where shopkeepers will round DOWN a bill.) Someone else fingered the silk flowers. A couple came in with their baby, stood around and left again, we wondered why. After 10 or 15 minutes of this Aristea rummaged around in an outbuilding for a box to gift wrap a wonderfully colourful tray of no apparent practicality. On arrival at a party, gifts are deposited casually near the door and are completely ignored by the recipient.

Aristea took us aside and whispered us upstairs. Out and up we went in the dark to large wooden locked doors. Zac, their youngest son who was in his bedroom, peeped out the next door (there are three, one on the other side of the house, too) and she dashed over to him to tell him to come to the OTHER door (10 feet away) to let us in the formal entrance.

We were obviously the first arrivals in spite of it now being an hour past starting time. Only Maria, Aristea's mum, was there helping in the kitchen. In excruciating embarrassment we sat and watched TV with Zak and chatted with Maria in our limited vocabulary for a very long time. The clock crept around to 10:15, 10:30, 10:40. We were offered in succession a hazelnut chocolate, a chocolate marshmallow thing, a hazelnut pastry covered in sugar and a small open tart filled with sweetened fresh cheese, mezithra.

Finally, others began to arrive, including eventually and astonishingly all the people we had seen in the shop. The couple with the baby were Albanian, one of a substantial number of families who have come to Crete for a better life. Albanians are distrusted and generally regarded with suspicion but Kostas and Aristea are both very kind to all us foreigners. The host himself was the last to appear and did not make an appearance until 11 pm when he closed the shop.

The same sweets in the same succession were offered to each new arrival but not to the others. There was laughter when one woman was offered them out of sequence. By this time there were about 25 or 30 people in the small house and only 12 places set at the dinner table. We were curious to see what would happen because it seemed impossible to accommodate the now enormous crowd.

The food was served about midnight and finally someone beckoned Aristea to add more places. All Cretan dining tables expand with extra leaves and a second table was also brought from storage so by midnight everyone was squashed in side by side except Maria (still in the kitchen), Aristea (who didn't have time to sit down) and the children, Nikos and Zac (who hovered in the background and ate on the run).

After the meal Kostas cracked open a bottle of Ballantine's whisky. He went round the table with it carrying a single glass, with which each person was expected to toast Kostas and his day and toss back the small amount of whisky. Kostas reciprocated. The glass circled the table and those who couldn't finish their portion poured it out on their plate. The entire bottle was drunk, almost half by Kostas. Kostas looked white and exhausted at the beginning of the party after his 15 hour working day but rose like Lazarus, rallied by the company and the drink. People continued to arrive long after everyone had finished eating. The food was still on the table, congealing and cold and it was passed to these newcomers, who accepted it enthusiastically. There was no fussing about reheating the dinners, hot food is not especially appreciated in Crete.

Suddenly the house was attacked! Gunshots erupted within meters of us. The loud reports reverberated through the house. Paula screamed and dived under the table, to the entertainment of all the old hands. Just the Cretan method of celebrating, nothing to worry about. Every few moments a man would step just outside the door to shoot the sky and swagger back in ostentatiously tucking his pistol into the waist of his trousers.

One of the most engaging distinctions between these celebrations and our birthday parties is that, rather than acting Lord of the Day, the celebrant uses the occasion to show appreciation of his friends by serving them. At a saint's day celebration of a wealthy man he bustled around the taverna the entire evening, acting as waiter, ensuring that plates and glasses were never empty and offering titbits of meat at each table. Being opulent in both pocket and waist, he was manifestly exhausted by the end of the evening.

CHAPTER NINE

Toil for Oil

Scott Davies NINE

Vineyards and olives surround the village in a patchwork of alternating bright green vines and grey-green shady groves. These two crops form the main occupation of the village, and also provide the only source of cash income for most of the inhabitants.

Young vineyards cover much of the surrounding hillsides and valleys. Early in the 1990's Crete was devastated by phylloxera and most of the crops in Heraklion district have now been replaced. There is no effective treatment for the disease except the drastic cure of ripping up the ancient vines and re-planting, after resting the field for at least a year, with phylloxera-resistant stock from California. The desired grape variety is grafted on to the wild root stock after one growing season. This process means that the grape harvest is lost from each vineyard for four to five years while the new vines are developing. By 1995 the new vines had generally become established and the arduous work of replanting and staking had been completed by most of the area's farmers. The significant loss of income from one of their only two crops has meant great hardship for villagers in recent years and will only be made up once the vines are several years old and producing to capacity.

In most of Crete the preferred variety is one of the sultanina types, such as Thompson Seedless, used for making raisins. Raisin growing came to Crete with the Greeks from Smyrna during the great population exchange with Turkey in the 1920s. In summer bunches of grapes are spread on the ground or strung along racks to dry in the sun. These wire racks are a common roadside site, although for most of the year their purpose is not obvious. The sun-drying method is said to be far superior to factory drying as practised, for example, in California. The process is not quite as pure as we first thought, since prior to hanging the bunches on the racks they are immersed in a solution of potassium salts. This chemical cleans the grapes and accelerates the drying process. During the week or so the grapes are drying the man of the house will sleep outside among them. We were told that this is necessary to prevent theft. The raisins are marketed through the village co-operative, but every household has their own supply carefully stored in sealed bags together with a few bay leaves or cloves.

Although Crete can not claim to be the world's first in producing wine, archaeological evidence from 4 000 year old grapes found at the Minoan site of Zakros provided proof of the first grape cultivation specifically for wine. Furthermore, finds of wine making equipment there indicated that the Minoans were technically the most advanced in wine-making techniques. Thus, the ancient assertion that Crete gave wine to Greece and ultimately, Europe, is borne out.

According to Miles Lambert-Gocs in "The Wines of Greece", Cretan grapes have traditionally provided Greece with almost a fifth of its wine and Crete is reputed to produce the finest dry reds. Almost all Cretan wines are produced by co-operatives. The Eastern province of Sitia, which includes Zakros, is still one of the major appellation wine areas of Crete. The grape variety grown there is liatiko, of such antiquity that it is considered the ancestor of the Corinthian grape used to make currants in ancient Greece. It's name is shortened from iouliatiko, from July, indicating it's early ripening properties. These grapes are also grown in the nearby Dafnes region. The red wine from these grapes is bottled under the name Malvicino. Wine from liatiko is a peculiar and unique orange colour, especially in the homemade versions.

Arkanes and Peza, the largest wine producing cooperatives in Crete, prefer a blend of two other grape varieties, kotsifali and mandilaria, which ripen in mid September. Peza also produces white wine from the vilana grape, bottled under the name Regalo.

Two retsinas are produced in Crete; Domenico (named after El Greco, Domenikos Theotokopoulos) is made in Dafnes from vilana and rosaki, which is commonly preferred as a table grape; and Ekavi (after another ancient name for Crete) from Peza, made from vilana and sultanina. Retsina has been described as a "try-anything-once" wine and is generally not spoken of in polite oenophilic circles. We, however, drink Ekavi in great quantities (literally, it has the curious property of never inducing hangovers).

Every village household annually produces a few hundred kilos of wine from its own grapes. Red and white grapes of various varieties are blended, stomped, fermented and poured into their wooden barrel, mixing with the previous vintage. In this way the barrel is never emptied and the new wine is modified by contact with the old. Thus the concept of vintage is not known here, they call wine from old barrels "old", even when it is mostly this year's.

We had heard that the sweet malmsey or malvasia wine, which was so popular in Britain from the 13th to 19th C, derived its name from its origin in our district, Malevisi, in Crete. We had, however, also heard that claim being made for a similarly named area in the Peloponnese. Lambert-Gocs' book explains that the name came originally from Monemvasia on an islet off the Peloponnese, but not all malmsey wine came from there. As demand increased, the Venetians began producing it under the same name in other areas under their control and Crete became the most significant producer and shipper. Malvasia wines were mostly whites and were produced from numerous varieties of semi-aromatic grapes. Since the 19th Century, interest in malmsey wine has died out and it is no longer produced commercially.

Many of the houses in the village have a "crevatina", which is a large frame, made of wood or metal, upon which vines are trained. These crevatina cover the avli or the balcony. Apart from providing a ready source of fresh table grapes they also provide very welcome shade in summer.

When we first moved into our house there were three ancient vines planted in the avli and trained up the side of the house. Since no crevatina was provided these grapes just grew all over the flat roof of our balcony, and most were spoiled by rotting or insect damage. After a few years of wasted harvests we decided to install a crevatina. Manolis the Taverna recommended we use Stavros, the local welder and fabricator. Manolis came himself with Stavros to plan the construction, trim our existing grapes and plant three additional wild vine stocks for later grafting. The serious planning and negotiating finished, the session turned into a rollicking party with everyone in earshot dropping in to join the laughter. One of the participants, we heard later, rolled home to be admonished by his wife for having forgotten to fast before taking communion the next day.

Having agreed with Stavros to erect the crevatina "next week", we waited nearly two months, the delay occasioned by Stavros' backlog of demand for iron stakes for the new vineyards. Our insignificant crevatina was well down on everyone's priority list. Nor was there much rush, since the grapes had just begun producing their first leaves when we agreed the job. Even by the time Stavros and his assistant, Antonis, completed the structure after two days hot, sunny work on the balcony, the vines were only just large enough to justify our self-important purchase of the official bright pink grape-tying ribbon for a couple of large cheerfully optimistic bows tied around the short stems.

After the grapes have been used to make wine there remains a large quantity of residue consisting of skins, stems, juice and pips. This residue is used as the raw material for making raki (also known as tsikoudhia), the Cretan version of aquavit, schnapps, etc. Manolis the Taverna came for us one afternoon and took us to a friend of his, Vangelis, who has a copper still in Agios Mironas. He also makes more wine than he needs for his own use so sells some to the taverna, and to us for home consumption. We buy ours in a 25 litre jerry can, the kind most people fill with extra petrol. When we lug it home full of wine, we get many offers to help empty it from the cafenion crowd. Sometimes, it causes a spontaneous party at our house!

We sat in the back of Manolis' truck surrounded by the smelly residue, slightly fermented after a month in large garbage bins, wood for stoking the still and potatoes for baking in the ashes.

The still is a very simple affair with only one 2" pipe coming out of the top and bending down into a primitive heat exchanger consisting of coils immersed in a cold water bath. A plastic bucket sat in a hole in the floor to catch the warm raki. Vangelis had an hygrometer to check the alcohol content but this is a mere formality. He can taste and smell the strength to within half a percent.

He is a strong hairy man of few words, compact and accustomed to humping large barrels. As we arrived he was just finishing another batch of raki and was opening the still. The solid residue was shovelled out to be used for fertilizer, ultimate recycling, nothing wasted.

Then our charge was poured into the still with water and herbal branches for flavouring. It took a mere 32 minutes to come to the boil and start producing, 10 minutes later a gallon of raki had been produced. The initial strength was 24% alcohol, by hygrometer and Vangelis' nose. The raki is aged for two minutes, then tasted with bread rusks but, in general, this initial strength product is kept only for medicinal purposes. After another 20 minutes the raki was being produced at about 20% strength. Production continued for an hour when the concentration had reached about 13%. These various strengths were mixed to give the "drinking" raki of 17-18%. It tastes much stronger.

The rest of Vangelis' family arrived bringing wine while

Manolis barbecued brisoles to go with the baked potatoes and, as usual, the whole thing turned into a party. We recorded the afternoon by taking extensive photographs of all phases of the operation. A few days later we discovered that we did not have a film in the camera. Oh well, we can always do it all again next year!

The other main product in the district is olives, grown for home eating and commercial production of superb oil. Late in December one year, we had our first small taste of the life of olive pickers. The olive harvest had been going on for almost a month and we had been pestering our friends to take us with them to help collect the harvest. All the families go every day if there is no heavy rain, throughout all of December, January and February to pick up the olives as they drop from trees in the scattered groves. Curiously, everyone seemed reluctant to let us go with them and we were not sure if it was because they thought we would be bored by the extremely mundane chore, or if they thought we would be more of a liability than a help. In any case, we pressed the point in the taverna and more or less insisted that Manolis take us when they went out the next morning.

The church bells were just ringing 8 when we left the house. The school bus had passed and the upper square was deserted. Manolis was doing some final loading of bags and bowls when Maria came out dressed in a three sweaters, her ubiquitous skirt, with pyjama bottoms underneath and stockings beneath those. She was not to be defeated by the cold morning!

We drove to the bakery and obtained emergency rations of

sweet sesame buns. A multitude of primary school children were also stocking up for the arduous day ahead with fresh, hot buns. We drove to Ano Nisi, their ancestral home, riding in the back of the truck like real labourers were doing all over the island at that time of the year.

"Etho (here)", said Maria, signalling our arrival at the small grove. We clambered out, reaching for baskets and bags. We refused an invitation to coffee and hot buns since we had just finished breakfast and didn't need the agony of bending over picking olives on an over-full stomach. They led us up the hill to where their twenty trees were slowly dripping the annual crop. We asked whether we were to pick all of them, green, brown, black and blemished and Maria confirmed "ola (all)". So we began. The work is laborious, yes, but soporific too and accompanied by only the twitter of birds and the occasional languorous conversation about the quality and quantity of the harvest. No other chat is necessary. The work has the familiarity of long years of repetition, each person (except us) knew what was required.

Maria and Manolis tried to explain to us the differences in the varieties of trees. We were working under one which was two hundred years old. Its gnarled trunk spouts new shoots that Manolis must continually hack away with the mattock. Almost next to it is a sapling, only about 15 years old. It bears tiny green olives that Maria picked straight off the tree.

"Doesn't it matter that they are green?", we asked. No, it seems. The next tree she shook vigorously, releasing a cascade of gently plopping fruit. When Paula tried this on a neighbouring tree, she received a gentle admonition. The olives are best when black and to shake the tree releases the unripe and unready green olives. The tree that Maria had shaken was near the road and the olives, when they fell would have been crushed by the passing traffic.

We picked quickly as soon as we understood what was expected, although nowhere near the rate of Manolis and Maria. Manolis interrupted us only once, telling us not to pick facing downhill, it is more tiring. In the next couple of hours we forgot this advice several times and laughed at our own stupidity.

There are many things we didn't understand and we were full of questions our Greek was too rudimentary to express. Why, for example, do they not have nets laid down here, as we have seen in so many other fields? And do olive pickers, the seasonal workers from foreign countries, especially Albania, get paid by the kilo or by the day? Paula voted for daily pay, with accommodation and food and a small remuneration. Mike voted for payment by weight, for how else could you ensure that work is actually done in the field? We did not know, so we had no resolution; we could only pick and wonder, thinking that money would be poor reward for us. It was a fine day, the sun was shining, the birds were singing and if we were not picking olives we would be stuck in the dark back room of the house, cleaning the ceiling beams of 200 years of accumulated dirt and engrained filth. On the other hand, of course, we did not have to do it again tomorrow and the next day and the next day for months on end.

By 9 am we had already finished. Maria was surprised but these olives had been picked recently and there weren't many.

We had picked only one large sack. They seemed to assume we were ready to quit but we had hardly whetted our appetites and would feel cheated if we went home so early.

"Where next?" we asked and Manolis responded by asking us where we wanted to go. We thought that a silly answer, we wanted to go where the olives needed picking but Manolis and Maria were acutely aware that this was merely a tourist expedition for us and let us decide. Finally Paula suggested "Pano, pano (higher)" where Maria had said she preferred to pick and where the view is spectacular.

On the way we passed a ploughed vineyard. It was the vineyard which had once produced the grapes that we had eaten, now the vines had been savagely ripped out as it was infested with phylloxera. Some of those grape vines had been truly ancient, now it was a barren field and remained so until the dreaded aphid had been starved to death. Two years later new resistant vines were planted together with cherry, apple and apricot trees. Between the new vines a temporary vegetable garden was also planted. This is a way to maximize the use of the land while the vines are still immature and developing.

The second field was a similar size, about 20 trees. We parked and carried the baskets through another steep grove to the family's trees. It had seemed odd to us that Maria liked to pick in groves with a view, since most of the time is spent staring at the stony ground. Olive picking, however, is like all other village activities. The pace is slow, there is time to stop and enjoy the landscape. Maria quietly expressed her pleasure several times. She wore gloves because her fingers were sore from the hours of scratching in the hard earth. Having rejected her offer of gloves for ourselves, we began to feel our own fingers, but were glad of the contact with the soil and the smooth, round fruit.

These trees had not been picked recently and to collect the numerous olives Manolis had brought a contraption that looked like a lawn mower. It was an olive picker, called a "hedgehog" which consists of several independently rotating cylinders bristling with spikes. The olives are impaled on the spikes and carried to a metal comb which flicks them off into a waiting, detachable hopper. The mechanical hedgehog was apparently invented in Kato Asites by Patelis Frachiathakis. We have never seen it used elsewhere in the olive growing world.

Manolis "mowed" the carefully tended naked earth dotted with ripe berries. When the hopper was full, he transferred the contents to a larger basket and shook it vigorously until the leaves and rubbish had fallen out. We were impressed by the simple, efficient and labour-saving device which, unfortunately, cannot be used on the steeper fields. The machine is not perfectly efficient, however, and the thrifty farmer follows it, picking the few remaining olives by hand. It took us much less time to pick twice as many olives as in the first field. In total, we had picked about 80 kg in three hours which would make about 20-25 kg of oil.

Maria tried out our embryonic Greek with a new conversation. We caught the words, "today", "Kostas" and something else but as Manolis was quick to tell Maria, "they don't understand". Manolis tried next, "Kostas, Wa, Wa!"

making the instantly comprehensible sounds of a newborn babe crying. Maria simultaneously clicked in with, of all things, an ENGLISH version of "Happy Birthday to you" and we dissolved in laughter as we finally comprehended that it was Kostas' birthday. As far as we are aware this is the only English known by monoglot Maria.

"What time is it?" Manolis asked. It was 10 to 10 and Maria recalled that Kostas was born at 10 am. We resumed our picking and in a few minutes we heard the church chimes. "Hello Kosta" Paula yelled and Manolis chuckled his slow, easy laugh, both at the memory of the birth of a son, and at the confirmation of our comprehension of the fact.

We stopped picking in what seemed to us the middle of a field when Manolis crossed the road to collect under a new tree. Although we expected to carry on with the whole field, Manolis said the rest of the trees did not belong to him. It was a family inheritance, only one tree was his, the rest belonged to his sister.

An adjacent grove was overgrown with the olives unpicked and neglected. "The farmer died," said Manolis sadly, "and the trees are abandoned." He had children, but they have gone to seek a faster, richer life in Heraklion.

Growing among the olives and adjacent grape vines were wispy green fronds looking like young onions, "prassa" (wild leeks). Manolis and Maria offered us some after explaining how to cook them (with potatoes, tomatoes and olive oil). We explained that we eat leeks with ham in a cheese sauce or in soup but they didn't seem impressed. They then proceeded to dig up vast quantities and put them in a plastic bag for us. No trip to the olives is complete without collecting the day's quota of horta!

We rested at the foot of the field and enjoyed the fresh buns, apples and the magnificent oranges of Crete. The mountain seemed close enough to touch in the clear air.

Manolis claimed it was not worth picking any more olives that day, there were too few. He suggested we come out on a Saturday with Eugenia and Kostas, barbecue and make a day of it. They also suggested that we now go back to their house for something to eat and more overwhelming Cretan hospitality, but we refused. We gave our own work as an excuse and it was true. Rain was threatening after more than a week of sun and we were not sure that the house was yet rainproof. However, we had other reasons for refusing. We would like to be able to go to pick with them again and did not want them to feel they needed to stop their work to entertain us. We also suspected that, after we left, they went out again, to pick some more before the rain.

Surprisingly, on the way home, Manolis invited Paula to drive the pickup truck, while he sat in the back with Mike. When we were ready to leave she took her place at the back, thinking perhaps it has been another of Manolis' jokes, but no, he gestured her to the driver's seat.

"Do you know the way?" he asked, although there is only one road.

"No" she answered casually, driving off. Maria, in the cab beside the driver, muttered a comment about the wonderful things women are getting up to nowadays. There was a special satisfaction about that drive, passing surprised looks of the other farmers as they waved to Manolis in the back, staring at Paula in the front. When we arrived home she carefully negotiated the narrow gate and put on the hand brake. Manolis saw it was on and immediately assumed Paula had driven all the way with the brake on! What do women know, eh?

When the following olive season began we received a call from Eugenia, inviting us to go into the countryside with her parents. Although we were working on the computer, we said immediately that we would be delighted to go. It is always an education in things Cretan to go out with Manolis and Maria.

It was sunny and about 22 C, but Maria was bundled up in trousers and sweaters; we were dressed only in t-shirts. Cretans believe absolutely that flu and colds are caused by the slightest chill. Manolis and Mike hopped into the back of the truck, Paula drove with Maria in front. We went first to one of Manolis' olive groves up the mountain behind the village, near one of our favourite walks. There, among a number of small, young trees, there are two old ones with very large green olives, from which they pick the plumpest and finest as eating olives. We were instructed to pick as many as we wanted, straight from the tree.

Meantime, Manolis and Maria gathered the first of the season's fall from below the trees, along with some dried up fruit left over from last year. These olives, they said, make poor oil but they must be picked up first before the ground is raked and smoothed for the main harvest. It seemed unlikely that the return on effort would be worthwhile but here nothing is wasted.

Olives are graded by the oleic acid content. The best eating olives in the world come from Kalamata, on the Greek mainland, and have an acidity of only 0.05%. When pressing his crop for oil Manolis must decide which to keep for home use and which to sell to the cooperative. Usually the best, with an acidity of less than 1%, is kept for home consumption. At this level, the oil receives the designation "virgin" in the main exporting countries, France, Spain and Italy. Most of Greece's olive oil is exported to Italy, where it is blended and reexported as Italian olive oil. If the acidity is 4 or 5 percent, it is considered inferior although still edible, but anything higher than 10% is toxic. The leftover olives which have remained on the ground from last year have an acidity of about 15% to 20% or even more. Hence, the oil from them is used as a lubricant or for lamp oil.

When we finished picking a couple of kilos, which seemed like a lot of olives to us, we started to help collect the fallen ones alongside Maria. One look at our measly half bag though, and we were sent straight back to the tree for more. "Think of your friends, when they come to visit", they said.

"Why, Maria's brother Giorgos picked three full bags last week, just for his family!"

We explained as best we could that we didn't want to pick too many the first time, in case we ruined them all. We had actually already experimented on our own. On one of our evening walks we had picked a small selection of olives and stored them in brine. They rotted some weeks later!

Maria scoffed. "It's easy," she said. "Just crack them all with a rock, put them in water and change it every day."

"For how long?"

"It depends how sweet you like them", she replied. "Some people like them sweeter, some like them a little bitter. After 10 or 15 days, taste them to see if they are ready."

Having finished with these trees, we got back into the truck and drove to yet another small grove in Ano Asites, part of Maria's inheritance. We again passed many astonished looks from their friends who recognized Manolis' truck, but were surprised to see a woman driving and Manolis waving regally from the back. This grove consisted of a dozen young trees, about 5 or 6 years old. These ones were laden, and Manolis and Maria glowed with pride at the heavy branches dragged down by the weight of the olives. Mike was sent with Manolis to pick still more green olives; these were smaller and must be soaked separately, because they will be ready sooner. Maria and Paula picked radikio, a small, fuzzy leafed, white rooted horta with a pleasant bitter taste. It bears no resemblance to the Italian vegetable of the same name. It is cooked and eaten with olive oil and lemon, or raw as a salad. Prassa were also growing well here, and we picked a large bunch. Maria told us that the green stems are eaten, so we had wasted most of the edible plant when we had picked them the previous year. They thought Paula very dull witted indeed, Maria said the best part is the green leaves.

There were two other villagers picking horta in the same place, a mother with her grown son. Maria chatted companionably with Katerina as they gave each other tips on where to find the best horta. Manolis, anxious as ever to separate the sexes, called Mike over to admire the trees, then Katerina's son as well. Soon, the women were picking horta in a small group, while the men chatted a hundred metres away and Manolis' sense of the order of the universe was satisfied.

Once again Maria explained the procedure for cracking and soaking the olives. In case of language difficulties, she demonstrated by cracking one of the olives with a stone and then carefully searched for two stones of just the right shape and weight. Manolis suggested we use a small hammer, but Maria was shocked and vetoed the idea at once. Manolis backed down immediately, this was woman's domain.

As we wandered back home through the village lanes with our spoils, we were not short of comments and advice for their care and treatment.

One day we walked to the post office in Agios Mironas through a gathering storm. The south wind was gusty and noisy, roaring at our backs and blowing the clouds in all directions in the sky so that they seemed about to collide into each other as if on an atmospheric freeway. While we enjoyed the spectacle of clouds moving impossibly in opposite directions Paula's scientific mind was analyzing the illusion, appraising the phenomenon as a spectacular example of the Ekman spiral, in which wind (or ocean currents) change direction and speed as they approach a surface which acts like a brake, such as the earth or seabed.

On the way home the wind grew more fierce, not cold, but chaotic and disorienting. As we crested a hill it brought us up sharply to a complete standstill in a mobile world of flying dust and leaves and small plants. The olive branches were whipped around until the silver undersides of the leaves rimmed the trees with halos against a purple-black sky with an ominous luminosity. An olive pelted Paula in the knee like a black hailstone.

Near the cemetery we came upon two old women from the village, their olive sacks resting on a bank and consternation on their faces. We knew them, but not their names. They were returning to the village on foot and were frightened because they could not manhandle the sacks on their shoulder against the force of the wind and imminent rain. We took up the bags and began walking with them. Though half our size and twice our age they kept trying politely to relieve us of our burdens, muttering thanks to the Virgin Mary under their breath. Their expressions spoke of relief, deliverance and confident assurance that their god always takes care of them in their hour of need.

We had gone some way when the rain started. In seconds we were all soaked through. Safe now, and nearly home, they were able to laugh. We all giggled together.

"The rain is good," they said, "it was very dry."

"Yes, but better perhaps a half hour later," we answered and we all laughed again.

In the village we insisted on accompanying them a short distance out of our way to take the olives home. As we trudged through the wet streets they exclaimed aloud to everyone we passed, half the village was watching the first rain of the wet season from sheltered doorways.

"Look what good people they are", they shouted, "they are helping us carry our olives."

Among themselves they worried what they might offer us as hospitality, a cup of coffee, perhaps. The older woman struggled to keep up with us. She had no breath left to talk.

When we simply pointed to our soaking clothes and said we must leave immediately they could not protest but wanted to give us payment of a couple of eggs.

"Not a thing. It was nothing. We must go."

Spontaneously, the two women pulled Paula to them and embraced her on both cheeks. Bless you both, they said with radiant smiles that were blessing enough.

CHAPTER TEN

The Rural Life

One of our favourite walks is in the next valley at the head of a deep gorge. There is an old flour mill there, downstream from Ano Asites. Although overgrown now, it was still operational during the war when Michalis the Neighbour was a small boy and he told us the story of being sent to mill some flour by his mother, only to have it stolen by German soldiers on the way home. They had been watching him through binoculars, and waited until it was ground and ready for cooking. He said that during the war it was a common trick in Crete for the locals to spike the confiscated flour supplies with the white powder of a local plant. It gave the Germans diarrhoea and stomach cramps. Michalis was clearly reliving the incident from so many years ago as he mimed the stomach aches.

Three large grindstones, some dilapidated mill paddles and a slightly broken grain jar sit forlornly in and around the millhouse. The gorge protected us from the north wind and the day was warm and peaceful. Yellow autumn crocuses were blooming amongst the bright green hillsides covered in clover, a reminder of the saffron season now in full swing in Spain. There is rosemary growing wild here too, and we took a cutting for our kitchen garden.

After dropping down to the stream level, we refreshed ourselves with an orange from a small grove, crossed the river and climbed the other bank to the small church of Agios Antonius. It is partly built into a rock face and is in a state of some disrepair. Apparently a son of Ano Asites, now a successful Chicago surgeon, has promised money to have it repaired and painted. We have also heard that the European Community will contribute money to construct a path along the pretty gorge formed by the river. We selfishly dread the prospect of tourists in "our" gorge, albeit on a smaller scale than at the famous Samaria gorge.

While we were inspecting the church, a shepherd, dressed in black, with the Cretan headband and swinging his crook, passed by on his way to his flock. We greeted him and continued to the south side of Ano Asites in search of horta. Still not confident of our ability to distinguish edible from inedible, we picked only a very small amount. By the time we finished it was afternoon and the weather was turning. We made for home.

Back in Kato Asites we brought out our bag for inspection in Michalis' cafenion, to see if we had been correct. We were laughed at, because, although we were right in our selection of vrouves and radikio, we had brought home such a ridiculously small amount as to be not worth cooking!

Since those early days of tentative horta identification we have become somewhat more knowledgeable and often combine our daily walks with a collecting session. We can now pick a yield which would do any local housewife proud. City born and bred, Paula is highly appreciative of learning the ancient rural arts, which have already disappeared in so many places. There is a great, though totally erroneous sense of pioneering independence from the sophisticated modern world.

Our neighbours warned us not to collect under vineyards or

olive groves where chemicals might have been used recently. They said we could be poisoned, although we believed this to be an exaggeration. A few days later however, there had been several days of continuous sunshine and we noticed on our walks that many people were spraying beneath the olives and grapes. To indicate the presence of poisons, it is common practice to leave the empty bottle upturned on a branch or post. We picked up one of these and discovered it to be a deadly paraquat, so now we have more respect for the advice of our neighbours. The herbicide works by inhibiting photosynthesis in any green plants. After a few days treated fields are bleached white and look frost-covered and forlorn. Roots and soil are unaffected and the highly water-soluble chemical disappears rapidly from the system.

Continuous indiscriminate use of these herbicides, however, is robbing Crete slowly of the abundant natural wild flora. In a few years the magnificent displays of spring and autumn colour will disappear and Crete, like the rest of Europe, will have been sacrificed to man's misguided practices. It is absolutely insane to poison the vegetation, particularly since the dead material is plowed into the soil. Less fertilizer would be required if the mulch were added still green and useful and less erosion would result from leaving the greenery to absorb the water during the rainy season.

One beautifully warm and sunny November day we missed our daily walk altogether. We had spent the morning cooking a dish of macaroni with fresh tomato sauce, spinach, carrots, courgettes and cheese topping. This goes well indeed with the local wine, which we had also just topped up at Vangelis' house and we broached the first from our ersatz wine barrel.

We were happily slaughtering flies, which had become a daily preoccupation because they were a plague at this time of year. But then we began to notice the bees. They were acting peculiarly. In fact, they were acting drunk. We probably didn't register the first couple. The ones we noticed were slow and unusually easy prey to the fly swatter. After that we really began to take notice. There were three, all together, on the floor of the avli, buzzing, staggering, overturning and righting, trying to fly but not getting off the ground. One traversed half the width of the courtyard and then seemed to have a crisis on some particularly rough territory where it tipped over several times and had difficulty getting up again.

The bee incident, however, had really started much earlier when Mike was mixing cement in the avli and Paula was once again trying to stop the leaks in the verandah with waterproof sealant.

"Listen to those bees in the loquat," said Mike. "They are incredibly loud."

Paula agreed absent-mindedly and went on with the more important task of stopping water from landing on our meals. She didn't realize then that it would be the theme of our day.

Later during the bee incident, Mike said, "I've read about this. They get drunk on too much nectar and then they have to sleep it off before they go back to the hive."

We had been going to go for a long walk after lunch, taking advantage of the first sunny calm day in ages but it was impossible to quit the courtyard where the drama of the bees was being enacted. Paula called for more wine instead.

"You don't frighten me with more wine", Mike said, and went to get it.

"Look at him, look at him staggering around!" Paula shouted after him, in order that he shouldn't miss a particularly dramatic moment in the bee opera.

"Have you seen yourself lately?", he asked unperturbed and continued into the house in quest of refreshment. Paula fetched the camera to record the drunken throes and snapped away happily until the film was finished.

"Those photos will be little furry blurs," he said when he returned. There were only two bees left. One had flown off or disappeared.

"He's dead", said Mike of the remaining corpse, trying to put a damper on the drama.

Monty Python scripts raced through Paula's head. "No he's just resting", she murmured inaudibly. "No he's not, I just poked him and he moved," she retaliated sharply. "Try it."

Mike prodded the poor bee, which wiggled his toes and flipped over.

"What are you doing, leave the poor thing alone, let him sleep it off!," Paula shouted hysterically, in memory of innumerable hangovers of her own.

"I'm just trying to get him right side up again," Mike said calmly and continued to prod.

"Harassment" Paula shouted again, having bitter experience

of what she perceives as his sadistic streak, trying to get hungover people out of bed, where they are perfectly happy being miserable.

A third bee, meantime had curled up in an unnatural posture in a remote corner of the avli and had not moved for some time.

"This one's dead," Paula pronounced solemnly.

Mike sauntered over with his weapon and prodded it. It moved uncomfortably. "No, just dying", he said pessimistically. "What about our walk?"

"We have to see this thing through," slumping further down in her lawn chair with the freshly filled glass of wine. Mike began his usual defence against her immobility and sloth. He started repotting several cuttings he had collected earlier. He has a congenital inability to sit still. Having no such problem, Paula returned to her serious study of late season bees suffering the effects of excessive flower nectar.

Mike sighed. Paula heard him distinctly, as he contemplated the demise of his plan for the gorgeous sunny day.

Fortunately, the phone rang, and distracted him. It was our friend Sylvia calling from near Niagara Falls, Canada, where she moved for the good life and proximity to cultural events such as the Shaw Festival. We had barely made it to two such edifying plays earlier this year, after a particularly herculean feast around her swimming pool; it seems to us that life in Niagara-on-the-Lake is well worth living. After a brief conversation, however, she thought (diplomatically) that perhaps it might not compete with the scientific study of late season bees in Crete. We tried seriously to affirm this scientific truism and encouraged her to join in our scholarly pursuit via the soonest possible flight to Crete.

Several hours later, it was beginning to get cold again as the sun lost its force in the late afternoon and the avli was in shadow. Two bees were still alive there, one much livelier than the other. We put them both together on the windowsill and Paula blew on them to warm them with her breath. Both stirred, one crawled vigorously away, but made no attempt at flight.

"It's getting more active as I blow on it."

"He, He," mischievous dimples appeared on either side of his nose, "don't we all."

Alas, both bees were dead the next day. It was still sunny, so once Mike had dragged a very large immobile bee out of bed we went for our overdue walk. In order to avoid a repetition of yesterday's lethargy, Paula proposed we set out immediately and take a day off work (which often entails considerable noise and hammering). It was still chilly as we left, but warmed up quickly on the sunny farm lanes. We took along a plastic bag and knife to collect horta. As we passed our neighbour, Maria from Anogia, on her way to the olive groves with her daughter and son-in-law she looked extremely sceptical about the prospect of our foraging successfully.

"Do you know horta?" she asked, unbelieving.

"Of course". Paula exuded confidence, although she did

admit to limited knowledge of their favourite hangouts, which all Cretan women know from generations of horta gathering with their mothers. Women in Crete would never starve in a war. Most men, however, would feast until they had eaten all the sheep and goats, and even then they'd only know one way to cook them, roasted on an open fire.

After advice to take the right hand fork, we sauntered off, in the direction of Ano and Kato Nisi, the two virtually abandoned villages near ours. It was an enchanting morning and was hardly marred by the fact that all the roadside weeds conspired to look identical and we couldn't tell a radikio from a nettle and a leek from grass.

Our horta bag was meagre indeed, until we were rescued by other neighbours. Eugenia and Michalis took a break from the backbreaking work of picking olives to greet us and playfully suggested we come pick with them. She looked at our horta haul and scathingly dropped most of the weeds onto the ground. She said there's not much radikio around here, but there is lots of vrouves just under those olives. In a flash, she had plucked the knife from Paula's hand and picked more horta in 2 minutes than we had in two hours. We were so grateful we spent two hours peacefully picking olives with them, and snacking on pomegranates. When we were seriously flagging, they spread a feast of mouth-watering home-made goat cheese, olives, bread and left over pork chops. Michalis has one of the village kasani, stills used for making the raki. At this time of the year, most of their evenings are spent turning the neighbours' grape rubbish into firewater, to the accompaniment of brisoles, wine, music and company.

From Michalis the Kasani we learned, as we picked, more about the mysteries of "good" olives and "bad" olives. His early season olives made poor quality oil with an oxea (oleic acid content) of 12 or 14. It also seems that, paradoxically, the smallest olives produce the most oil, although not necessarily the tastiest. Villagers can distinguish the subtle differences in flavour of oils from different parts of the island. Olive oil from the Messara Plain is especially distinctive and looked down on with disgust by the mountain folk.

At about one o'clock we wandered off with mutual thanks and went home to clean the horta. On the way, we encountered Maria from Anogia again, she who was so sceptical of our horta recognizing talents. They were just on their way home and we showed them our overflowing bag. She was mightily impressed and we certainly didn't spoil our image by telling her of all the help we had received!

When we returned to the cafenion we found an itinerant craftsman was ensconced there, repairing old chairs by weaving new rattan for the seats. He had come by truck, bringing with him his tools and supplies and his whole family. His wife and children, ranging from babe-in-arms to teenagers, sat quietly in a corner of the cafenion. Either he had no boys, or they were too busy working to accompany their father. The man had been engaged in his craft for thirty years.

It must be a profitable trade. Every Cretan house we have ever been in possesses these bum-punishing, stiff-backed, wicker-slung wooden tortures, the same ones that make you squirm and send your lower limbs to sleep in every cafenion and taverna. The Greeks can sit in them for hours, apparently in comfort. Are they built differently? We have never seen a Cretan home with comfortable, sink-into-it-and-snuggle up armchairs and we are always amused at the suspicion with which our own soft couch is regarded by the neighbours. When older people visit us there is a polite scramble for the hardest seats in the house.

Villagers were bringing their old chairs from home for the craftsman to repair. Then they sat, as if they were in a cinema, watching a particularly slow-paced, but very serious drama. Judging by the crowd there wasn't much excitement in the village that day. Many of the men there didn't even have any chairs to repair, they came simply to observe.

He refused our polite request to photograph him in action, stating that he was craftsman, not a model. We had previously encountered the same, not unreasonable, response from a potter at his wheel. After a few moments thought, however, the master relented and gave his permission to take photographs. Most of the cafenion clients joined in the photographic session, adopting stiff but friendly poses for the camera.

One evening in early June we received another lesson in our continuing course on rural life. Ritsa dropped in with her brother Yannis the Shepherd and cousin Malama to ask us something. It was a rather formal delegation and their vocabulary was beyond our Greek. We knew they were talking about the next day, something to do with sheep and at first we thought they were offering to sell us meat. Once we were corrected in that, we concluded that they were offering us some live sheep, perhaps to keep for milking or to raise for meat ourselves. We refused politely but adamantly on the grounds that we travel too frequently and could not take care of animals. Malama whispered in Yannis' ear that the obviously thick foreigners didn't have a clue what was being said. After our final firm, "not tomorrow thank you, perhaps next year", they left looking a little crestfallen and saying "it doesn't matter".

The next morning after breakfast we settled down with our coffees, promising ourselves a quiet day. A curry was bubbling slowly on the stove. Ritsa's household was buzzing with activity. We saw the whole family passing back and forth in front of our open gate, carrying trays of food and drink to the truck.

Ritsa's Mum, Evsevia, popped her head around the gate and said cheerfully, "we are going up the mountain."

"Why?"

"To ...." Incomprehensible verb.

"What?"

"Hang on just a tick while I get Renna, she speaks some English."

A moment later Renna's face peeped round the gate and she said, in English, "We are going up the mountain for the sheep shearing. Would you like to come?"

"Ahhhhh." We finally understood and accepted with alacrity. In our stupidity last night we had refused an invitation to one of the best parties in the mountains and our first offer to watch the annual sheep shearing. No wonder they thought we were daft! We promptly turned off the curry, cancelled the rest day, put on our walking shoes, poured a few litres of wine from our jerry can and grabbed some ripe loquats from the tree. We were off.

Eight of us piled into the pickup truck with tables, chairs, food and wine all around us and bumped up the mountain track to the sheep pen and shepherd's hut at 800 m. The men were already hard at it and had shorn about half the sheep, which came streaming out of the pen into the sun, tinkling and baaing. They looked embarrassed (sheepish?) in their nakedness as they were driven to a field below the hut. Large plastic bags were filled with the oily shorn wool and the rest of the flock were driven down from the upper mountainside.

Two dozen men were clicking away efficiently with their old fashioned scissor shears. About half were at work at any one time, being spelled off when they took a brief rest. Several others caught the sheep, flipped them over on the mat in the shearing area and tied their legs, ready for the shearers as they finished and released the previous one. A few bleeding nicks indicated the less experienced shearers or momentary loss of concentration in the heat and noise of the shearing shed. The shearers ranged in age from about 13 to over 60. We watched one of the older men showing a young lad the technique. The flock is 300 strong and they were being turned out in their summer garb at the rate of 10 every 4-5 minutes.

The women meanwhile circulated constantly with water, soft drinks and refreshments to keep the shearer's strength up. A large sheep was sidelined by a swashbuckling Cretan pallikari-type with a handsome face and huge moustache, wearing a black shirt and his knife tucked into the waistband of his trousers. With a flashing movement he pulled the knife from his pants and slit the sheep's throat just outside the hut. As the sheep twitched in its death throes he kicked it and stood on its neck. No sentimentality in this crowd.

A pallikari is a figure that needs some explanation. He's a much admired fighting lad who can kill two Turks with one hand tied behind his back and leap Psiloritis in one bound. He does everything too much - bravery, stupidity or both. If he likes a woman he wouldn't be afraid to ride his horse right into her mother's front parlour and steal her. And he always, always has a large bushy moustache. You can say nothing more complementary to a Cretan than that he is a fine pallikari.

An admiring young assistant brought a long wire for him and he poked a hole in the hind leg. Kneeling down on one leg, the very picture of the triumphant hunter, he blew the skin away from the carcass before skinning and deftly butchering it. Women brought out water fetched from a spring a hundred yards down the mountain. The crude joints were tossed into a huge cauldron and boiled over an open fire. No spices other than salt were added. Rice was added to the remaining stock to prepare pilafi. As the stock was not fatty enough extra margarine was added. The party settled down gradually into segregated groups. Adult males from the family and their relatives stayed in the sheep pen. The young children ran and played outside, chasing each other up the mountain and into the old hut built into a cave in the mountainside. They photographed each other, standing in stiff poses with their best friend of the moment. Older children were sent off to pick oregano. During this season the plants are in flower and the blossoms are considered the finest part. Wild oregano picked from the high mountains in early June is a culinary delicacy guaranteed to elevate a simple pasta sauce to an elixir of the gods. It has a stronger, earthier taste than commercial oregano.

In the cool of the shepherd's hut, the women worked at one end, while the visitors and townsmen sat at the other, drinking raki and wine. While the mutton was cooking sweet bread, sheep cheese, mezithra, mezithra pies, loquats and the highly prized koukoretsi were passed around. Koukoretsi are the cooked liver and other offal and these are considered choice bits, with honoured guests being served first.

Grandmother was present, dressed in a long black dress, black stockings and black headscarf, circulating in the 30 C heat of midday. Seen from near her face was shockingly young, almost unlined. Her husband had died, her children have children and she is constrained in her role as aged grandparent, sacrificed to the needs and whims of the younger generation, though barely middle-aged herself. For some women this is a rewarding time of life, freed from some, at least, of the hard women's work, which is now the burden of the daughter or daughter-in-law. Still, it must be hard if a woman is widowed very young, as has happened countless times in Crete's turbulent history. Some such women become bitter and complaining, lording it over her son's wife. More commonly however, grandmother is quiet and diffident and greatly loved by the small children and spends most of her time helping the next generation of women to raise their children.

People were arriving all during the morning and early afternoon until the party made up about 70 people. We tried to sort out the families. The owners of the flock, our neighbours, have seven children. They are among the few people in the village who still live entirely as shepherds. Their cousins, also from Kato Asites, have five children. Another branch of the family had eight children in the parent's generation, six of whom were present with their children. Many had driven from Heraklion and looked out of place in dressy, town clothes.

An odd incident happened as the crowd was drifting about enjoying the day. A man arrived who was no one's relative. He had hitched a ride or walked up the mountain. His approach caused a buzzing among the young children playing outside. In a flash they disappeared, hiding behind their parents in the hut. The man was not quite "all there", either retarded or with some mental problem. He had not been invited but was courteously welcomed. He stayed, mostly isolated and silent in the corner where he was periodically offered food and drink. He kept trying to press some kittens on us, saying they were cats from the jungle and would be 7-8 kilos when fully grown. We were not sure whether they were real or a figment of his imagination but we did not want them. When the shearing was finished the men emerged with the last of the sheep, tired and dazed from the dusty, oily, thick atmosphere of the shearing shed. They had been shearing many hours, their hands must have ached from repeated closing of the shears. Not a few would have blisters the next day and at least one had a long bleeding gash in the thumb. The food was ready and people piled into the shepherds hut, or ate under the shade of the cliff. Great piles of mutton and heaps of rice and macaroni were served with lashings of bread and fresh cucumber and tomato salad. Wine and beer, still cool from immersion in the spring water were passed liberally. The conversation slowed and became somnolent as people were tranquillized by the heat, the food and the wine. There was no energy left for dancing to the cassettes of Cretan music. In the long shadows of the late afternoon the women quietly began cleaning up. The drive home was subdued and contented. After a wash up at home Mum came over for a tired coffee in our courtyard with Ritsa, Maria and Renna and cousin Malama who had lingered with them. The other girls had orange drinks but Malama accepted the offer of beer and enjoyed it hugely, to the stern displeasure of the others. She was pressured not to finish it, it being unseemly for village women to enjoy drinking too much. Besides, Malama was only 13.

The next year we were invited once again but that year there very nearly was no shearing at all because there were no sheep! In early spring the boys went up to milk the flock and couldn't find them. Wandering up the mountain they soon determined that 70 of the flock of 90 sheep had been stolen during the night. The family were devastated! It represented a loss of most of their cash income from cheese and meat and a good part of their capital, millions of drachmas in all. Manolis and the boys wandered for days looking for their branded sheep among all the neighbouring flocks and finally found them above a village about 10 km distant. They confronted the thieves. Manolis the Shepherd doesn't exactly look the part of the ferocious Cretan pallikari. He has a moustache alright but he is kind of rolly-polly and jolly and doesn't look like he could ever hurt a lamb, never mind a lamb thief. But to our astonishment the girls reported to us that the thieves confessed in fright and gave the whole flock back. The police were never brought in and everyone was satisfied, they had dealt with the predicament themselves and solved it, as in the old days, by themselves.

CHAPTER ELEVEN

Home Cooking

Few gourmands would come to Greece for the food but Cretan village cooking is more than the monotonous array of moussaka, souvlaki and Greek salad offered by the tourist tavernas. Although it does not have the inventiveness of, for example, Italian cuisine, meals in Crete are seasonally varied, healthy and, at their best, delicious. We have tasted dishes in houses of our friends that have never appeared on restaurant menus, being thought too countrified and unsophisticated. Wild snails, whole sheep's heads, pikti (pig's head and feet jellied with lemon and orange juice, a Christmas delicacy), stuffed courgette flowers, pilafi (rice cooked in stock), homemade lukaniko (sausages air-dried or smoked by hanging in the chimney) and several varieties of fresh and dried beans are all regulars on village tables. Homemade spoon sweets made from quince, figs, cherries, raisins, mandarins or tiny, whole, bitter oranges are always available to welcome visitors. In the old days ashes from the wood fire were included in some of the traditional sweets.

We enjoyed a dish made from burghul (cracked wheat) which, we were told, is very old style cooking. Burghul also features in a dish made by shepherd families in the summer. Sheep milk is left to curdle and then boiled with burghul for several hours. The resultant mash is eaten at once or laid out to sun dry in small clumps. During the cold winter nights it is eaten like porridge with milk and sugar and is said to be very warming.

One of the distinctive features of Cretan cuisine is its ancient heritage. A catalogue of the food remains and references to crops found at Minoan archaeological sites reads like a present day list of Cretan ingredients. Wheat, barley, peas, chick peas, sesame, almonds, cumin, coriander, fennel, celery, mint, olives and olive oil, honey, figs, quinces, pears, grapes, wine, cattle, sheep, goats, pigs, fish, octopus and possibly chickens were all eaten 4 000 years ago. Judging by the degree of innovation in the preparation of food they are probably still being prepared in much the same way as well. Water birds, wild deer and boar were hunted in ancient times but were driven to extinction or near extinction in recent historical times. The only common innovations of present day cuisine are tomatoes and potatoes, New World plants which arrived after the invasion of America by Spanish Conquistadors.

The wet season staple of the village diet is horta. There are reputed to be 52 varieties of edible plants in Crete, not including a similar number of herbs. One day we received an advanced course in horta collection, which substantially expanded our repertoire and elevated us to the status of barely competent. It came unexpectedly and very suddenly.

We had been helping Eugenia with her English lessons, prior to writing the extremely difficult University entrance exams, and one day her parents came to have lunch with us after the lesson. We chose a highly conservative menu with great care, as this family do not hold with mucking food up in fancy sauces and confusing tastes. The discussion at lunch came round to the subject of Maria's famous horta pies, hortopittes, which are made with her unique pastry and are filled with the deliciously subtle flavour of wild fennel. It is rather rare and patchy in distribution, perhaps because, according to Polunin in "Flowers of Greece and the Balkans", it sometimes escapes from cultivation. Maria, however, knows where to find some and after lunch we piled into their truck to pick it.

We went first to her now deserted ancestral village, where her grandparents had a house. Then we turned on to a farm track and drove slowly for a long time while Maria scanned the roadsides. Apparently in the middle of nowhere we stopped. Suddenly she bent down and began to attack an almost invisible green speck in the ground. Maratha, wild fennel, our goal. After a while we too learned to pick it out from the high erect dead flower stems from which the new growth was emerging. We would certainly have never spotted it on our own.

After a beautiful sunny morning, the weather began to turn in the late afternoon and the wind howled around the steep slopes, reminding us that winter was not yet finished. Eugenia was getting chilled but Maria was oblivious, walking and bending and exclaiming as she found other new varieties of horta. For hortopittes the wild fennel is one of the most highly prized finds. It can not be used on its own, however, so she was also searching for others of the correct type to mix it with. We picked, in all, more than a dozen different kinds. Most were impossible for our amateur eyes to distinguish and we began to get the impression that anything you pick up on the roadside is satisfactory for boiling and eating. We were soon disabused of this naive notion, though, when Paula picked some for inspection by Maria's critical eye. "Nothing", she said, "those are flowers."

Manolis disappeared down an apparently vertical cliff, picking handfuls of fennel without even bending. While we rooted around almost in one spot he disappeared at his deceptively leisurely pace into Maria's brother's olive grove for a quick inspection. After picking large bags of fennel Manolis and Eugenia began to drive slowly back while we walked with Maria along the road looking for one particular kind of horta which Maria had not yet found. We were confirmed in Maria's original eagle-eyed spotting since the fennel plants petered out almost immediately.

Nearing the abandoned houses again we turned off toward an old church where there are some laurel trees. Maria uses bay leaves to keep raisins fragrant, putting a couple of dry leaves into each half kilo bag. She says this is about all she uses them for. We picked them for soups and stews and when we got home we threw them fresh, straight into the chicken stock we were making from the lunch leftovers. The rest we washed and laid out to dry.

In the evening we tried to make sense of all the varieties, sorting them into different bags for each type, keeping one plant of each to press for future reference. Maria said she would give us a call when she was ready to clean and prepare them, so we wanted to be ready to write the names of each and the uses to which they are put. Some are for pitta, some for boiling and some for salad. She would also teach us how to make the pittas.

The next afternoon we received the call from Eugenia that Maria was ready to start. We hurried down to the taverna with our sorted bags of horta, ready for identification and instructions for use.

Maria took us into the kitchen where she was surrounded by the horta she had picked yesterday, some cleaned, most still waiting for the preparations. The first step was to clean the wild fennel. Each small shoot was delicately picked up and examined for old or damaged stems. These were removed and the good bits placed into a large bowl. Curiously, Maria dropped the rejected parts back into the uncleaned horta bowl, which made sorting increasingly difficult as the ratio of rejects to unsorted fennel grew. This is, however, how she cleans all her horta, often sitting with the bowl in her lap, watching the world from their balcony. As she worked Maria would mutter softly, "this one is dry", "this one is good", "this one is no good". Her criteria were a mystery to us, we could not distinguish or predict the good from the rejects!

After sorting, Maria placed the bowl under the tap for numerous washings. Each time, the bowl full of horta was filled with water and then the vegetables were swilled around and lifted out carefully into a second bowl. The first bowl was drained and the bottom checked for dirt, bugs, etc., as a measure of progress. The horta was apparently ready when no dirt was left. Next, all the shoots were picked up by the base and aligned in batches for cutting into lengths of about 2 cm. During the handling of individual shoots Maria checked them again for flaws. Like most women, she never uses a chopping board but cuts the vegetables straight into the bowl, pot or pan from her hand. As she worked Maria explained other uses for wild fennel. It is especially favoured with potatoes, cooked in the same fashion as wild leeks but is also cooked with beans, hake, cuttlefish and squid. She seemed a little doubtful when we said we eat it with lamb, but admitted the possibility. Since the collection of wild fennel often coincides with Lent, it is not surprising that meat does not feature strongly in these dishes. Labour-saving, cultivated fennel can be bought in the shops but Maria prefers the wild variety, which has a stronger fragrance. All the fennel is used as leaves, we have never seen the large, delicious bulbs so often eaten in Italy, although we can't imagine why they would not be as well suited to this bit of the Mediterranean. The dearth of fennel bulbs must be attributed to culinary rather than horticultural reasons.

When all the fennel was finally cleaned it was put into a large pot with an enormous quantity of oil, between 1 and 2 cups. About the same amount of water was added, the pot was covered and placed on the highest heat on the stove, where it cooked for half to 3/4 of an hour while the other horta was cleaned. The cleaning is very time consuming and Maria explained that she picks a little every day when she goes out to the olive groves. When she gets home she cleans it and puts it in the fridge, where it will last for five or six days. In this way, she avoids having to spend too many hours cleaning horta at any one time.

After seeing the amount of oil used to cook the fennel we asked Maria how much the family uses in a year. "About 400 kilos", she said, "because of the taverna". Only their own good olive oil is used, she said, for frying chips and for the salads. They never buy what the Cretans call "seed" oil, such as corn or peanut.

While the fennel was cooking, Maria carefully selected fronds from the mixed bag of other species to achieve the right balance of sweet and bitter. Each plant was scrutinized, flowers and old leaves removed and tough and dirty stems cut off. When all was ready and washed there was about twice the volume of the fennel. It seemed like a lot but Maria said it cooks down to nothing. When the fennel was soft and ready the rest of the horta was added with a little more water a large amount of salt and the pot was replaced, covered on high heat. It was cooked for about half an hour more and then turned off to cool. There was no water left, only oil.

During this natural break in the proceedings Maria topped up the wood stove with more fuel and went outside briefly to throw away the rubbish and bring in some walnuts. A stone was fetched from its home under the sink for cracking the shells. She put the plate of cracked fresh walnuts in front of us, to munch while we watched her work.

It began to rain and Maria expressed her satisfaction, not as we thought because the olives needed rain, but because she had been out to the fields many days in a row with the recent good weather. She said she was very tired, and so was Manolis. Also, she says hot weather is bad for the olives, which make better oil in cold weather.

Next the dough. The making of pitta dough is a matter of great pride for each woman and all have their secret variations and tricks to make theirs both special and infinitely superior to other women's. It is made with oil, water, a little salt and enough flour to produce an elastic but pliable dough. Maria's secret is to add raki, which makes the dough easier to handle and produces the right texture. Others add lemon instead of raki, said Maria, but it makes the dough tough.

Small balls were rolled out into circles and a large spoon of horta placed on each. The circles were folded in half and cut with the edge of a plastic bowl. Maria trimmed the edges carefully to be sure that there was no extra dough without filling. After making a few individual circles Maria then demonstrated some variations, including rolling larger pieces to make several crescents at once. Another variation is to fold a little of the edge up and pinch them together with the fingers. This is called "hand-made", said Maria.

The traditional Cretan shapes for hortopittes are called "boxathakia". A square of dough is rolled and the horta is placed in the centre. The edges are then folded in forming a smaller square. This shape uses more dough for a given amount of horta and is less favoured nowadays.

For company Maria makes smaller pittas in round shapes using a cooky cutter with fluted edges. She made two of these fancy small ones "for Eugenia".

If there is dough left over after all the horta is finished Maria makes plain discs of dough to be fried and eaten with a little sugar. She and Manolis like these but the kids prefer them filled. Altogether she made 27 hortopittes, each about 10 cm, and four plain discs. By the time she was ready to fry them she had been working for almost four hours, and this does not include the time taken to pick the horta. Making hortopittes, said Maria is a full day's work: to pick the horta, clean it, wash it, cut it, cook it, make the dough and fill it, then fry them.

Just as she began to fry them Kostas, Manolis and Eugenia appeared as if by magic. We ate the hot pittas as they came out of the frying pan, as fast as Maria could cook them. The raki makes little bubbles in the dough when it hits the hot oil and saves the dough from tasting oily. In a few minutes, the entire day's work had virtually disappeared.

We were too tired and too full after the cooking lesson to bother with our own supply that evening. The next day, however, as we were munching the pastries Maria had given us to take home we boiled a large pot of water and cooked a few fronds of each variety separately so we could taste them individually. We made notes on the pages of the pressed specimens of which ones were bitter or sweet and which we liked best. We particularly liked the red-stemmed "wild radikio", of which mostly the base and stems are eaten. We discovered that the bitterness can be eliminated by changing the water midway through cooking. They are then very nice as a cold salad in French vinaigrette.

CHAPTER TWELVE

Incense and the Evil Eye

TWELVE

Like most villages in Crete Kato Asites has plenty of churches. Most of the village people are extremely religious, of the Greek Orthodox faith mixed liberally with a strong element of more ancient beliefs and superstitions. There are ten churches in and around the village, ranging in size from the immense Agia Triada (Holy Trinity), dominating the village from above, to our local church, the diminutive Agia Paraskevi (Saint Friday) which is the oldest in the village. Since they are all Greek Orthodox, and Papa Yannis is the village's only priest, only one is in use at a time.

The rest of the churches are only used on the relevant saint's day, with normal services rotating among Agia Triada, Agia Paraskevi and Christos, (Christ Church) which is the main village church in the square. The services are interminable, lasting sometimes for 5 hours, many people only start to get ready once the bells have been rung by the priest and turn up when the service is in full swing. There are only a few seats provided for the old and infirm with most of the congregation informally standing up, moving around, greeting neighbours and going out for a smoke break.

In spite of the plethora of village churches there are another seven or eight within easy walking distance, another five or six in the next village, Ano Asites, and two in the Nunnery Gorgolaini, which stands just outside the village on the side of the mountain. This is a very famous, old monastery and is extremely beautiful with its' ancient cypress and plane trees and a sacred spring of fresh water. The magnificent cypress is reputed to be the oldest in Crete. Although there are no longer any nuns resident a lone, young monk is based there and holds regular services for the public. On special occasions, such as Christmas, Lent, Easter, etc., there is a steady stream of well-dressed ladies strolling up the steep hill, or being ferried up in cars, vans and even mini-buses. The monastery is a frequent stop on the Greek religious tourist route. The monk provides small cookies to any stranger who wanders into the monastery grounds to enjoy the tranquillity of the place or take a drink of the refreshing spring water.

Although many of the country churches are only used for services on one day a year even the most obscure, decrepit looking ones seem always to have signs of devotion. People pop in to kiss the icons of saints, light the votive lamps and candles, make a small offering. Cautious mothers importune their children to kiss the air above the feet or photo, lest they catch germs. One of our nearby churches, Agios Pandaleimone, (the healing saint), is located right on the overhanging end of a high plateau with magnificent views over large parts of central Crete. This is only reached after a long walk from the nearest villages but always has candles burning nonetheless. This is also one of the churches where people who are sick hang small tinplated or silver symbols embossed with the part of their body that is troubling them, eyes, arms, baby, etc., and ask the saint to help cure them. There are strong parallels between these offerings and the findings in Minoan cave and peak sanctuaries, where people offered gifts to propitiate the gods and make special requests.

An important component of church services is the sung liturgy. A cantor, similar in function to the cantor in the

Jewish religion is a separate and highly esteemed position. We can hear him most days since services at our corner church are hooked up to a loudspeaker for the benefit of those in the neighbourhood who don't make it into church. One day we serendipitously received a lesson in this music at a taverna on the main road near Dafnes.

The owner of Taverna Gonianis was retiring to bed while we were still sipping the last of our wine. On his way past he stopped to say good night and we asked about the two books he had under his arm. They were texts of Byzantine Church music and he opened them to show us a whole new world. The writing looked like Arabic with chopped up Greek words beneath it. Byzantine church music is based on the same octave scale as European music. Instead of the five-lined notation with notes, treble and base clefs we are familiar with, however, it is expressed in another language. It had never occurred to us that there may be several musical languages, just as there are spoken ones. At the top of the piece the key and tempo were notated in analogy with andante, allegro, etc. The key may change several times during the piece and each change is signalled in mysterious symbols among the horizontal and vertical curves, apostrophes and marks. One or two short strokes above the symbols indicate extra length notes, such as half or whole notes do. The sung lyrics are written below each "note" with, for example, "Kyrie" taking up perhaps a whole line of sung text.

Orthodox church music is a specialist field and our friend had been studying it for more than five years. He sang some excerpts for us in a melodious, rich tenor, following the music with his finger to show what the symbols meant. Curling strokes up or down indicate the familiar sounding sliding scale and he showed several places where the key changed briefly before reverting to the original. The keys seemed to be named up to four and then start again with a second set of four to make up the octave. Do re me, are thus named first, second and third "sound", in literal translation. We were absolutely riveted to our seats listening to him give a simple and lucid explanation of the music he loves.

Religious activity is not confined to church services. Many people kiss a priest's hand when they meet him in the street. Most women and many men cross themselves as they approach or pass a church and small flurries of repeated crossings pass like a wave down the seats on the local buses, signalling the passing of some (sometimes nearly invisible) church or important shrine. Greek Orthodox christians cross themselves by touching forehead, breast, and right, then left shoulders, making it backward to the Catholic sign of the cross. Travellers also cross themselves several times at the beginning of a journey and have tremendous faith in the gesture. One time we offered a lift to a young friend, who made the sign of the cross as we pulled away.

"Aren't you going to do up your seatbelt?" we asked.

"Oh no, we are not used to doing it," she replied casually, "we make the cross instead."

There is nothing abstract or remote about religion to these people. Tales of the saint's adventures are learned along with their own family history. St. Paul's shipwreck in Crete and his eradication of poisonous snakes from the island really happened, perhaps during their grandmother's time. A walk with the girls from across the lane gave us a graphic illustration of the solidity and literalness of their faith.

Ten of us went for a walk to Kastella Rock, the four girls from across the lane, Mike's sister, her husband (also Mike) and their two daughters. The rock is a protruding limestone plug near Gorgolaini Monastery projecting about 20 to 30 m above the surrounding slopes. Solution features in the porous limestone on the top trap rainwater into small seasonal pools teeming with insect larvae and water plants. Paula was last up the steep slope, while the young girls cavorted on ahead. When she got to the top the four Cretans were engaged in a heated debate and shouting at us to come over.

"Pola, Pola, ella etho (Paula, Paula, come here)."

"It was right here," said Ritsa in an authoritative voice, but Malama broke from the group and ran over to another steep precipice a few metres to the west.

"No, it was here," she shouted to the others, "come here quickly". The girls ran over and peeked timidly over the edge. They conferred briefly and agreed. "Yes, yes it was this spot," and then they launched into an exciting story about the rock which had apparently happened a year or two ago.

"This is where he threw the leondara, (lion) off the rock and killed him," they told us.

"Lion," we said, "what lion?"

"Well, it is sort of like a lion, but with a very long tail and fire coming out of its mouth."

"Who killed it?"

"Agios Giorgos."

Ahhh. Apparently, this rock was the very spot where St. George slew the dragon and the girls were showing us the very precipice where the beast was tossed off the edge. The girls almost remember it themselves. They believe that St. George actually strode across that rock. As proof, they pointed out his footprints in the small pools.

When we got home we had a discussion about the episode with Carol and the family. "That's silly," said Mike, a Catholic, "everyone knows that St. George and the dragon are from England."

Few weeks pass without some saint's day or special event in the religious calendar. The first day of each month is celebrated by drinking holy water from the church, or sprinkling it in the corners of the house to keep it safe from evil. Many of the religious customs still bear the hallmarks of their more ancient roots, marking seasonal festivals of fertility and harvest rites which date back to Minoan times. Since the schism between the Catholic and Orthodox churches in the 11th Century, the Orthodox church has retained more of the earliest Christian rites with, for example, the climax of the religious calendar at Easter, not Christmas. Although Christmas is celebrated on 25 December, Easter is a variable holiday celebrated later. Thus, the Greek Orthodox religious calendar differs from both the Russian and Roman ones.

Unlike the Catholic and Protestant churches, there are three arduous periods of fasting annually, 40 days before Easter, the first 15 days of August, before the feast day of Christ's mother and for 40 days before Christmas. During these fasts meat, eggs and dairy products are prohibited. With a bewildering complexity of rules, olive oil is also not used on certain days or on days when communion is to be taken, although vegetable oil is not prohibited and may be used. Fish is not eaten during most of the Easter Lent but is eaten during the early days of the Christmas fast and oysters, squid and lobster are approved anytime. Most of the women strictly observe the regimes, the men are much more perfunctory, on the grounds that they are working hard in the fields and need their strength. This implies that the women do comparatively little, which is far from the truth. It is just another example of the inequality of the society.

It is a curious feature of the Orthodox religion that priests must be married while monks, bishops, etc must be celibate. Thus, there is absolutely no hope of "promotion" for the village priests and apparently little effort and time are expended in their education. In some cases a six week course is enough to qualify them. We find this a curious system, whereby the most ignorant and superstitious of the clergy are in closest contact with the large body of the faithful. Our village priest, Papa Yannis, is absolutely typical of his class with long hair and beard (they are not permitted to shave or cut their hair) and very large belly. He is reactionary even by orthodox standards and forbids menstruating women to set foot in a church, an old-fashioned bit of misogyny impossible to forgive. "Progressive" priests impose no such ban.

Blood features in other guises as well. After ritualistically eating the body and blood of Christ communicants believe that to bleed would constitute a careless rejection of him, so they take special care not to jeopardise themselves in any situation where they might get scratched or cut.

Surprisingly to us, in view of the relations between Greece and Turkey, the Patriarch of the branch of the Greek Orthodox church to which Crete responds is located in Constantinople, which is what the Cretans still call Istanbul. The head of the rest of the Orthodox church in Greece is in Athens.

The bells of Christos accompany many of our waking and working moments. From the village square the lowest of the three notes peel the hour and half hour (one ding) through the day and night. All three chimes toll the services for all the feast days, Sundays, holy days and saint's days. A repetitive sequence of five chimes on a single note calls the children to Sunday school. On Christmas morning they wake us before dawn for the 5 am service.

Many of the common saint's names in the village occur around Christmas and New Year, Manolis (Emmanuel) is, of course, Christmas day, Saint Eugenia is celebrated on Christmas Eve, Yannis (John) is 7 January and Vasilis (Saint Basil) is New Year's day. On Saint Basil's day the priest walks around the village accompanied by Saint Basil and children singing carols. Saint Basil, both here and around the Heraklion shops, looks remarkably like Santa Claus or Father Christmas. As they pass through the various parts of the village people give offerings of money and receive the priest's blessing.

January 6th is the date of Christ's baptism, fota. Shops and offices are closed, church services take place virtually all day, starting well before dawn. People dress in their best clothes, and on this date the village priest blesses all the houses in the village. As the priest goes from house to house he is accompanied by the local children who sing carols as they go around the village. Since ours is a fairly large village with many houses to visit, reinforcements are called in from Petrokefalo, a village some kilometres distant where they have fewer people.

The priest is offered some nuts, sweets, fruit and, usually a glass of raki, at each house. On the evening of one such day we happened to be sitting in Michalis' cafenion drinking raki when Papa Giorgos, the Petrokefalo import, came in from his rounds. He went around the cafenion offering his cross to be kissed and slapping each patron lightly in the face with a sprig of wet basil. Since we were near the front we were the first to get such treatment. When we were surprised by a sprig of pungent, wet basil hitting us in the face and a gold cross being thrust into our faces for kissing, we hesitated briefly between our strong anti-religious views, and decorum. Good manners won out and we performed our veneration, albeit probably unconvincingly.

Dashing back out the door and leaving his minions to collect the cash offerings, he said he'd be finished soon and would come back to join us for a drink. This was irresistible to us, as we had been extremely curious about the clerical species but to date had never so much as exchanged a word with our own Papa. Papa Giorgos staggered in with great dignity after half an hour, plunked his great mass down at our table and asked for another glass to join us in our raki. From amongst the folds of his untidy and none too clean cloak he brought out the booty of his hard day's work, oranges and sweets. He generously offered them around and toasted us, speaking a few words to each person in the cafenion and trying to get as many as possible to join our swelling company. He chatted away to us in a mixture of Greek and English and invited us to visit him in his village. We found him loud, inclusive, exuberant, emphatic and likeable. After a few rakis he stood up and asked for the bill. Michalis the Cafenion waived all talk of payment dismissively (as Papa Giorgos knew he would) and our new friend and unsuspecting ambassador for the clergy wandered off somewhat unsteadily.

During the three weeks prior to Lent the village celebrates Carnival, similar to the more grandiose carnivals of South America. The origin is claimed to stem from the ancient spring orgy and festival of Dionysius, the god of wine, so it is also an opportunity to savour the local product. During this period there are many celebrations, parties and dances, giving an excuse to eat lots of meat prior to the Lenten fast. The children and some of the adults dress up in costumes to look like pirates, English ladies, clowns, butterflies, etc.

As part of the Carnival Celebrations every year a dance is held in the taverna in aid of school funds. On one of the occasions that we attended the admission charge of 2 500 Drx included brisoles, salad, bread, fruit and unlimited, excellent white wine from Siva, a village in the next valley. Also provided was the music with the village trio supplemented by a man playing what looked like a bongo drum with an amplifying horn at its' base. The usual dancing took place, somewhat inhibited by the presence of large numbers of children in their carnival costumes.

There were raffle tickets on sale at 200 Drx each for a variety of small, donated prizes. Those tickets unsold at 11:30 were auctioned off to the highest bidder. Nearly all of them were bought, at inflated prices, by the village president. Such largesse must be part of his price of fame. Our president at that time had been married to a nice village woman before divorcing her to marry Marina, a member of the Greek royal family. Aristea, who knows everything, told us with some satisfaction that he still pays alimony to his ex-wife in the village. Someone else denied this. After the draw was made at about 12:30 we said our farewells, the party continued until around 4 am.

On clean Monday, the first day of Lent, the village office is closed, no bread is baked and people eat a special flat bread called "lagana".

March 25th usually falls during Lent and is a big holiday for two reasons, one secular, one religious. It is the anniversary of the Greek War of Independence which began in 1821 with an uprising against the Turks and also the date celebrating the Annunciation when archangel Gabriel came to the Virgin Mary to tell her about the coming of Christ. It is one of Lent's two "days off" when fish is permitted. Since this is a national holiday there are parades in most towns and nearly all the stores are closed.

On Palm Sunday there is even more than usual church activity, bells and singing. It builds all week to a non-stop cacophony on the big weekend. During this holy week "beggars" pass through the village, taking advantage of the extra religious feeling by entering the yard to ask for olive oil or money, giving in exchange good wishes and a muttered, Cronia Polla (many years). The beggars are always women in black and are reputed to be foreigners and "gypsies".

On Good Friday the funeral bells toll all morning to commemorate Christ's death. However, it is business-as-usual and ordinary village life continues. In the Agia Marina graveyard there is a lot of activity with people, mainly women, tending and adorning the tombs, arranging flowers and walking around the tombs carrying burning incense.

Church services continue through Saturday augmented by loud fireworks and gunfire. Ano Asites sets up a 6 foot high red egg in the square. Tourists strolling along the main road back to their coach, are a reminder that Easter also marks the beginning of the tourist season.

At midnight, the climax of the Greek religious year, the bells sound for the service that signals the resurrection of Christ and the end of the 40 day fast. Easter Sunday morning is particularly quiet after a very noisy night. Many of the men leave the village early to start fires in the countryside that will cook the traditional Easter lamb. One year we received a telephone call from Eugenia inviting us for lunch. Walking through the village the smells of meat cooking were everywhere, all the people were dressed in their finest and fireworks were in noisy evidence. Barbecuing lambs had sprung up in gardens and on any patches of open ground. Courtyards were filled with people and the square was packed with strange cars.

We arrived at the home of Manolis and Maria to a round of

Cronia Polla and a glass of raki with a mezithra pastry. We sat on the verandah and drooled over sections of lamb cooking on fires in the ground opposite. Eugenia was making a necklace of lemon blossoms to hang around the picture of Agios Giorgios when they attended the service at Gorgolaini that evening. April 23rd is Agios Giorgios name day but since it coincided with Easter that year the celebration would be postponed until the next day. Lunch was ready at around 2 pm but before we settled down to it Eugenia had to take some to her aunt and uncle farther down the road. This couple lost their young adult daughter many years ago and have since effectively given up living. They never go out except to make regular visits to their daughter's grave or for essential business, many of their meals are sent down by Maria and Eugenia spends a fair proportion of her limited spare time sitting with them in perpetual mourning. The uncle, who can sometimes be seen walking down the street with a dignified expression under his flowing white mourning beard, has been trying to persuade Manolis to take over their olive trees in exchange for a proportion of the oil they produce. It's all very sad and, to our eyes, incomprehensible.

When Eugenia returned we went into lunch, in the kitchen as usual. Manolis and Maria have a nice large lounge/dining room at the front of the house but it is seldom used. There was one other Easter lunch guest, Maria's mother from Ano Asites. She's a grand old lady and a favourite of ours. She is also in mourning for her husband who died several years ago and she does not go out to public functions or parties.

Lunch was, of course, lamb with roast potatoes and lettuce salad. This was followed by fried rabbit and more mezithra pastries. They then passed around red painted hard boiled eggs and we each had to hit our neighbour's egg and see which one broke. The champion, un-cracked egg, belonging to Eugenia, is kept until next year, they brought out last year's champion to show us.

Children are baptised into the Orthodox faith anywhere between about one and six years old. The responsibilities of a godparent are significant and accepted as a great honour. They are chosen with care as they become "family" upon taking up this role, so much so that marriage is forbidden between a girl or boy and the child of their godparent.

The ceremony is long and complicated and a tremendous ordeal to the child. It involves submersing the naked child in water then re-dressing it in new baptismal robes. The priest chants over it continuously while it is paraded around and around, screaming at the top of its' lungs. Finally the priest takes the child and holds it up in front of the altar screen for a last benediction before offering up his face to kiss the important icons. Following the ceremony most families throw a party at which guests receive small pin-on crosses or emblems and commemorative gifts to take away.

Wedding ceremonies are often raucous occasions but are a little anticlimactic since the engagement establishes the two as a couple. An engagement is a serious commitment and the affianced couple are allowed almost complete license. Indeed, it is not uncommon for engaged women to become pregnant, which often signals that it is high time for the wedding. (It is thought nicer for the wedding to take place before the child is born.) Rings are exchanged during betrothal ceremonies and are switched from the left to the right hand after the wedding. Thus, a woman with a ring on the fourth finger of her left hand is engaged, if on her right, she is married. Dowries, though illegal, are universal.

During the wedding ceremony, headbands joined by a string are placed on the bride and groom's heads and then exchanged, signalling that they are now one. This is the "crowning", the pivotal element of the wedding and it leads to a common but confusing gesture made by most people when they want to mime marriage to foreigners. The Cretan makes circles round his head and then rapidly crosses his hands one over the other. Before we knew the word "gamos" (wedding) or had attended a ceremony we were very confused by this, since Cretans do not know that this ritual is not part of all wedding ceremonies and their signals meant nothing to us.

One day the bells were tolling the slow, eerie, haunting and relentless toll for the dead. The first time we heard this toll we knew instantly what it was, though no one had explained it. The day before an old woman who lived alone across from the taverna died; we knew because we went out for dinner and the taverna had closed out of respect. Anticipating the warmth of the wood stove, a pork chop and the gentle company of our friends, we instead returned home for a meagre sandwich in our cold house, a minor inconvenience compared to the woman's life according to the story we were later told. The woman was widowed and 86 but she did not die of old age. She was set alight by her own wood stove, in front of which she was huddling for solitary warmth. She was eventually found and taken to hospital in Heraklion, where she later died of burns and complications.

Ritualized customs play their final role in death. The first notification of a death in the village is the toll for the dead but many other signs follow shortly. The cafenia and shops buzz sotto voce as the information is passed on. Who died? How old? What of? With astonishing speed posters appear on village poles and walls with details of the deceased, all surviving family members and time and place of the funeral.

The body is laid out at home by the village women and a night-long death watch is kept by the close family. The body is washed and dressed. If a girl dies before she is married she is dressed as a bride. If the deceased has made a pilgrimage to Jerusalem to be baptised in the River Jordan, he is dressed in the baptismal garments which have been kept for the occasion. During the day friends visit to view the body and offer their condolences. Usually within 24 hours the funeral takes place. With incense swinging, the priest and altar boys proceed to the house and accompany the coffin and funeral cortege on foot back to the church.

The bodies are placed in the family tomb for about five years until they rot and the bones can be removed to the ossuary, a rather untidy, small building filled with stacked boxes of bones. Three and nine days after the death small sweet buns are blessed in the church and given to relatives and friends. Several additional memorial rites take place after 40 days, 3 months, 6 months, 9 months, one year, and on every anniversary. During the first 40 days the spirit is thought to be able to see and visit the relatives. After that time, the spirit is free. It is considered very bad form to forget the subsequent anniversaries, when offerings must be made in the church. In addition, there are two days annually of remembrance for all the dead, when women visit houses offering a small dish of wheaten sweet, mixed with glittering silver candies of the sort that decorate ornate cakes. A spoonful is placed onto a plate brought out for it by the householder who says let God forgive his/her sins. One year we had two visitors, young Maria was remembering her grandmother, old Maria her father.

On one of our walks through Ano Asites we came upon an ornate coffin propped up in the street against one of the walls. A wake was in full swing with a group of men sitting outside one of the houses eating the funerary feast and the sound of women chanting from within. Alongside the door stood an ornate multiple candle holder, borrowed from the church. The coffin had been parked down the street until it was needed.

Strict rules govern behaviour and attire during the mourning period. For the death of a father or mother mourning black is worn by women for at least a year and they do not attend public parties or celebrations. Men usually wear black for a month or so or opt for a black arm band instead. One of our villagers is one of Crete's most famous traditional dancers. When his father died a few years ago he dressed in black and did not dance or teach for a full year, a considerable sacrifice since that is how he earns his living.

Once her husband dies a woman is condemned to widow's weeds forever. We nearly made a significant social gaff when we inadvertently put the photo of a recent widow on our village display in the cafenion. Fortunately, the sensitive Eugenia spotted it in time and we replaced it. The woman thought it would be unseemly to have her photo shown in public so recently (a year or two) after her husband died.

So it is that the church pervades the entire lives of the village people and most of them do not question it but, in fact, gain great strength and comfort from it. As with most religions, the church is supported most rigorously by the women. Yet women apparently suffer most by it. Juliet Du Boulay has written a detailed and perceptive thesis on her study of a mountain village community in Evia. Her lucid description of the cruelty and humiliation inflicted on women by religion is stomach-turning; men are associated with all that is Superior, Right, Adam, Intelligent, Strong Minded, Cool-headed, Brave, Reliable, Strong, and Responsible; women are Inferior, Left, Eve, Unintelligent, Stupid, Credulous, Fearful, Unreliable, Weak, Sensual and Irresponsible. Furthermore, men are perceived to be "purer", "cleaner" and "closer to God" because they lack the ability to menstruate. (Let's not beat around the bush here, your average Greek male wouldn't win any awards for his sensitivity and enlightened attitude toward women.)

Our fellow villagers cannot conceive of the idea that we are agnostics and do not believe in a god. We have had many discussions on this with village friends, who use the conventional arguments to try to convince us. Or, more accurately, they try to trick us into admitting that we secretly do believe, since absence of a creator is anathema to them and, from their reactions, is in some way threatening. Our lack of religion undermines our status in the village and we are afforded less respect than if we were regular church-goers. Our friends think we will eventually come round, if they spend enough time talking to us. Usually they begin with the cliched argument that a superior being must be responsible for all this wonderful life on earth. Eventually, almost everyone brings up the story of a miracle which they have never personally witnessed but which they know is true because they know someone who saw it. These stories are much more interesting to us than their proselytizing. Some typical examples of local miracles are:

Years ago a teenaged girl got a spasm in her right arm, which remained clenched to her breast. No one could cure her and she spent several weeks with this painful convulsion. Finally a priest told her that there was a church near the sea where the saint would fix her up. Since the family had no car they walked for days to the south coast, over two mountain ranges. Finally they arrived on the hillside overlooking the church and when the girl saw it she made the sign of the cross three times - with her RIGHT arm. The problem never recurred.

A man who was having major problems he could not solve put a letter into a bottle with some olive oil and tossed it into the sea on the north coast of Crete. Several weeks later he received a letter from a famous church on the island of Tinos, thanking him for his note. We have been told that if we do likewise we will also receive a response. No comment was made as to whether the man's problems were solved as a consequence of receiving this miraculous response.

There is a church on the island with a small font. On the eve of the saint's day every year many monks and people go there to pray all night. Some years, and the last time was within living memory, the font fills with water and everyone may take a small amount for blessing without it becoming depleted.

One of the villagers told us he had been to this church but had been unlucky as that year there was no water.

Running parallel with formal religion is a more ancient and mysterious belief that appears to be universal in Greece, "To Mati", the Evil Eye. All pervasive and omnipresent, the Evil Eye must be warded off continually. Although normally invoked from thin air, it is also housed more specifically in certain people. There are said to be at least two old women and one man in Kato Asites with the Evil Eye. These people must be placated and it is not advisable to catch their glance. As evidence, we were told a story about one of them commenting to a man on the way to his fields on his lovely donkey, which then tripped.

The Evil Eye is especially malevolent toward infants. For the first 40 days of life they must be guarded carefully, bundled up to immobility (even in summer) and never taken out of doors. Even for adults, however, the Evil Eye is a danger and can be invoked by a seemingly harmless compliment. Fortunately, it is easy to take out insurance by spitting. Thus, if you make a flattering comment you must follow up with, "Ftou sou". In English the conversation might be translated as, "You look pretty today. I spit on you".

It is easy for the uninformed to be taken unawares. One day we were helping young Zacharis with English exercises at his home above the shop. His mum, Aristea the Shop, explained that Zac had just had his locks shorn in a very untidy cut by the priest at Gorgolaini Monastery, with the other boys in his class, in another of the many unexplained and bizarre religious rituals. Once the English homework was completed we idly complimented Aristea on her lovely basil plants and watched in astonishment as Zac spat repeatedly in every direction. Aristea watched him unconcerned although she is normally strict about his frequent breaches of good manners.

Later, when we asked our friends about this, they said he had done it that the plants might not wither. "They would not die ... well, they MIGHT die", said a nine year old Greek Australian girl who was fully indoctrinated into the old beliefs although it was her first time in Greece. Ironically, basil plants are grown near most doorways specifically to ward off the Evil Eye.

CHAPTER THIRTEEN

*R*IDING THE MINOTAUR

Not so many years ago everyone walked out to their olive groves, vineyards and vegetable plots and carried their produce home to the village at the end of the day. If there were particularly heavy loads to carry a donkey would be used. In the 1940's a three-wheeled truck with a small two-stroke engine started gradually to supplement donkey transport. These vehicles were made in Heraklion under the trade name of Minotaur, the mythical bull monster said to live underground in the Knossos labyrinth. Cars and trucks were unheard of in those days, as recently as 15 years ago there were only 5 or 6 in all the village. Today many families have one or more cars or pick-up trucks which are used as general transport and farm vehicle. For really heavy work, such as ripping out old olive trees or deep ploughing the stony soil a heavy earth mover is rented. This heavy equipment is also used to split the huge olive tree roots for fuel.

There are, however, donkeys still in regular use in our village. They are usually ridden by men. They pull the beast up to a rock or fence and stand on it beside the patient animal. Then with a twist and a humpf they are up, side-saddle, off to the fields with their feet beating rhythmically against the animal's side to keep it moving.

One day Paula became more intimately acquainted with donkey know-how. We were just sauntering down to the village square on our way to town. Around the corner a donkey came trotting, trailing a rope with a tuft of bush. It had obviously escaped from its tether and was taking advantage of its freedom to go wandering. We stood in front of it to try to stop it. It came to an uncertain halt and, against Mike's advice, Paula stood on the rope to try to catch it. Of course, it just slipped out from under her, nearly sending her head over heels in the process. The donkey didn't even notice the slight tug. About this time another man came riding down the road on his donkey.

The newly arrived donkey was urged close to the runaway while the rider waved his stick and shouted stop commands in donkey Greek. His mount became excited and uncontrollable, rearing and bellowing with rage and frustration, the din was earsplitting. A severe beating on the nose was required to bring it back under control. The runaway paused briefly and Paula grabbed the trailing rope. Between frantic attempts to rein his mount the look on the man's face was priceless: mingled horror, disbelief and an urgent desire to communicate words we would understand. Underlying all th is, however, was clearly outlined the philosophical mirth often displayed in Greece when the locals are confronted with the more peculiar excesses and eccentricities of foreigners. It was too late, however; in a split second the errant donkey was off again and for a moment Paula thought it had taken her hand with it. Now she realised what the wise old countryman had wanted to warn her about. It is not possible to stop a runaway donkey! Still shaking his head, the donkey rider continued slowly down the road, the runaway trotted on into the country.

We carried on to town, Mike driving while Paula writhed in pain from a sprained and rapidly swelling finger. We made our first stop the supermarket, where we hoped to buy a package of ice to ease the swelling and bruising. The store didn't sell any, however, so Paula went to the frozen food section and extracted a small packet of frozen shrimp, carrying it around while we did our shopping. Then as Mike was paying the bill at the checkout, she sneaked back to the frozen foods and stealthily replaced the only slightly thawed shrimp.

Although the pain was horrendous for a couple of days and Paula was incapacitated for any serious work the worst part of the experience was the embarrassment of explaining around the village the cause of the bandaged finger.

Although the vehicle that has largely replaced the donkey bears the Minotaur brand name, in the village they are more commonly called by the generic name mechani. Steering by the elongated bicycle handles is very positive and they are the only vehicles which can negotiate the sharp turns and narrow streets of the village. They can also haul phenomenal loads at a speed slightly faster than a walk and can tackle, precariously, all the rocky and steep tracks to the fields.

Most still date from the post-war years and none are younger than 30. They are a vanishing species in the Cretan countryside as they disintegrate and are replaced by pick-up trucks. The majority look their age although occasionally you see one whose proud owner has added flourishes like an enclosed cab, headlights or a new paint job. Our village garbage collection used to be made in one before the advent of wheeled bins and a small compacting garbage truck.

We had often seen them around the village and wondered what they would be like to drive. Close, if surreptitious, observation had revealed that the vehicle is started by sitting on the bench seat, wrapping rope around the flywheel, and then vigorously standing up and pulling with gusto. In the macho stakes there is considerable loss of face if your mechani doesn't start first time. Numerous levers and pedals are kicked or pulled apparently at random in response to the load and the terrain. To stop the engine short the power supply on the frame. The parking brake can be found at the edge of the road, a rock under one of the back wheels.

One morning, just prior to the arrival of our goods from Canada, as we were starting the work on the house that we had planned to do that day, Michalis the Neighbour, turned up at the gate. He wandered in in his usual fashion and announced by shouting in Greek and by gesticulating that today we were going to clear out the apothiki. This building was virtually full of dirt, rubble, concrete blocks and general garbage going back who knows how long. Before tackling the inside, Michalis started removing the rocks bordering the base of the lemon tree and hacking away at the soil around it. Paula just managed to save one of the two mint plants that we had put in there a few days before. He told us we should remove the rocks and put a nice concrete border around the base instead.

It had been many years since the 12 foot high doors to the street had been opened, the hinges had gone and their base was buried a foot deep in soil. We exposed the base and propped up the sagging wooden lintels enough to be able to drag the doors open. The marvellous mechani was parked right outside and Michalis started to shovel.

He indicated that Mike should join in by passing over a

shovel. It was also made apparent that this was men's work and Paula should disappear from the scene. She went back to sanding the bedroom floor, which was our planned job for the day. Mike stopped shovelling once he thought the mechani was full but was urged on by Michalis until the poor machine was groaning. When every new shovel load fell out as it was loaded, Michalis jumped onto the seat and shouted at Mike to remove the parking brake. As it rolled away down the hill Mike ran after it and leapt on. The mechani coughed and spluttered and slowed to a crawl at every hill but eventually reached the local dump near the monastery. All the rubble was shovelled out and dumped over the side of the hill. The return journey was much faster, coasting most of the way. Coasting in a mechani is a lot like riding in the front seat of a roller coaster, but without the hand-rail. It is absolutely terrifying with nothing to hold on to while you hurtle through space swaying alarmingly at each bend.

The loading, shovelling, coasting and hurtling were repeated six more times during the morning and the temperature was beginning to tell. At mid-morning Michalis asked Paula to make coffee, which she did, abandoning her own tasks to serve the needs of the men. Not a role she plays well or willingly.

During the next trip Michalis let Mike drive. All went well until the moment of gear changing i.e. pull lever "a" and kick pedal "b". The thing died. Michalis explained that the carburettor had been flooded by Mike's gross incompetence. They parked and pulled up the seat. Inside were various plastic containers, rusty tools and dozens of ancient spark plugs. Michalis took out the existing one and replaced it with an equally decrepit one from the collection. He then went through the starting procedure without success. He tried another plug, or maybe it was the original one again. Still nothing. After about half an hour he realised the machine was out of petrol. Needless to say he did not show remorse for blaming Mike in the first place but Mike was never allowed to drive again, thank goodness. Michalis poured some liquid into the tank from one of his plastic bottles, laid the plug on top of the block and produced some incredible explosions by pulling the starting rope. He then replaced the plug and they set off again.

Around mid-day Michalis announced a pause, which was just as well since we had to return a rental car to Heraklion by one o'clock. We thought we had agreed to finish the job the next day so boarded up the doors to the street and headed out to Heraklion. We returned from Heraklion in the afternoon to find the apothiki doors open with the mechani filled with rubble outside. Michalis came out of his house and indicated it was time to start work again. Another sweltering five or six trips, with intermediate excavating with the mattock and the room was cleared, except for the debris filling the wine press. Michalis recommended that we knock it down and shift that too. We declined, hiding our smiles. The wine press was cleared in another six loads a few weeks later at a similarly inconvenient time. But we could now actually move in the room and start using it to store supplies and tools.

Paula's first mechani experience came a few weeks later. While we were having a coffee, waiting for the office to open so that we could pay our electricity bill, Michalis suggested that, it being cherry season, we go with him to pick some. We agreed enthusiastically. There was a short delay while he sent Paula back in to change out of her good clothes and then we all set off in the mechani.

A rope tied across the back at about knee height provided both a hold and a kind of impromptu seat belt. Mike and Katerina sat on either side of the central driver and their daughter Aphrodite sat in the back with Paula, the appropriate place for women.

With a tug on the fly wheel and the still mysterious kicks and pulls at an assortment of unknown levers, the mechani set off with a groan. In a quiet word Mike had warned Paula to tuck in her knees and elbows around the corners, as there is often millimetres to spare (- and sometimes less, we now know what keeps happening to the downspout we have unsuccessfully tried to place at one of the narrowest parts of the street!)

Michalis was very confident on the well-known streets of the village and tore down the hills, careering around corners with what seemed to Paula, the green newcomer, like a death wish. Mike was sanguine, however, and said Michalis was driving very sedately, compared to when there are no women present. Notwithstanding his extra precautions, his wife kept up a constant soft chorus of "siga, siga, Michali (slowly, slowly Michali)". Her warning was based on experience since Michalis had rolled his mechani as he was driving down a steep country track. He had wrenched his shoulder and avoided more serious injury only with great luck.

On the steeper and rockier roads past the monastery the mechani slowed down of its own accord, and required continual attention with kicks and pulls. It is not clear whether these are strictly necessary or whether they are cultural remnants of the monotonous prodding with which farmers used to encourage their donkeys up the hill.

The cherry trees were a few minutes walk at the end of the road. There were 3 or 4 trees in a level place on the hillside, set amongst the grapevines, olives, onions, tomatoes and artichokes. Water is pumped to all the carefully tended fields through a succession of elderly, loosely connected hoses. The fields are rocky and the soil is very poor, ideal for these classic Mediterranean plants. Hours of backbreaking labour with very little mechanical assistance is required to coax the production of any garden vegetables. Donkey owners have one advantage over mechanized farmers - the donkey contributes a small return on the investment of his feed in the form of increased soil fertility.

To someone who grew up in Saskatchewan, with its miles of flat geometrical wheat fields stretching to the horizon on all sides, these fields seem romantically chaotic. With no geographic features for a guide, the fields in Saskatchewan are laid out in a north-south grid, with cross roads at exactly one mile intervals. Paula used to fly by them, without the need for a compass. In Crete, the hills, cliffs and rocky outcrops determine the size and shape of the fields and village streets and even after repeated forays she is continually getting lost.

We picked an enormous crop of cherries, thinking we were helping with the harvest, only to discover to our acute embarrassment when we arrived home, that the cherries were being picked as a gift for us. Katerina tried to offer us the two gigantic baskets of fruit, which would have taken several years to eat, and it dawned on us that we had probably caused them to waste a good deal of the crop. We had blundered again.

Most mechanis are unlicensed vehicles and for longer trips people take the local bus. On one occasion we were on the first bus going to Heraklion and it became held up by traffic in Agios Mironas. In fact, cars and trucks were "parked" where their drivers happened to have stopped them. The bus driver made the supreme effort of sitting with his hand on the very loud bus horn. In one of the vehicles blocking the road, a farm truck, sat a young boy of around ten years old and an older man, presumably his grandfather. The father was probably in the shop buying a packet of cigarettes. It is not thought necessary to pull over to park when stopping for cigarettes.

When the lad realised their truck was causing the problem he slid over into the driver's seat and started the engine. Barely able to see out of the windscreen and reach the pedals at the same time, he gingerly inched the vehicle through the narrow gap between the bus and the vehicle parked alongside him. Just as he was squeezing through, the owner of the vehicle came out of the shop and saw his pride and joy being inched through a tiny gap. His face froze in absolute terror. He ran after the truck waving his hands in the air and shouting at the top of his voice. He caught up with them just after the boy had successfully completed the manoeuvre. Not waiting for the truck to stop the man opened the door, shoved the boy along the seat into the grandfather and took over the driving while cuffing and berating his son who presumably thought he was helping the family out of a difficult situation. The grandfather took no part in any of these proceedings and merely sat there observing it all along with us.

Most of our bus journeys are not quite as exciting as that, in fact they are generally pretty boring. However, a trip made by Paula alone just before Christmas left a bad and atypical impression. The bus was full of school children going impatiently to the last days of classes before a two week break. A student down sat beside Paula, with the respectful "good morning" Cretan youths reserve for their elders even though her true attention was taken by her school mates. They were boisterous and cheerful, as they normally are only on their homeward journey.

At Agios Mironas they left the bus in droves and although it is then normally almost deserted, there was still an unusually large crowd of Christmas shoppers. The man who next sat beside Paula was noteworthy in several respects. In the first place, there were still other seats vacant on the bus and it is very unusual for any Cretan to sit with a stranger of the opposite sex. In the second place he did not greet her. She thought perhaps he noticed Paula's foreignness and was uncertain about language. She should not have so readily excused him, however, because no self-respecting Cretan lets a small detail like language barrier interfere with his hospitality and courtesy toward strangers.

For many kilometres Paula was wrapped in the vision of the sun-lit, snow-clad mountains. In a great cleft between the peaks the full moon dangled large and cold, a jewel between Crete's breasts. In the foreground bright green clover carpeted the ground below the twisted trunks of the trimmed grapes. The grey green olives were stiff and hunched with frost.

At each curve she felt the pressure of her seat companion's arm and moved politely away. After several turns she noticed, however, that there was nowhere left to retreat to. Suddenly, her attention was dragged from the magnificent scenery and focused sharply on the stranger. He was elderly, with grey hair and moustache. He was wearing his "going to town" suit, which smelled of mothballs and spoke as eloquently of infrequent use as did his obvious discomfort in wearing it. His hands bore the dark stains and blackened fingernails of the olive farmer in picking season. They were crossed in his lap, but his elbow, pressed against her arm, was awkwardly thrust out, rigidly immobile. His leg crept slowly across the seat, using every thrust and toss of the bus to aid his advance on Paula's space and body.

Her mind was in turmoil, wavering between two worlds. In one, she was the sophisticated international travelling female who regularly encounters such surreptitious sexual assaults, laughing them off. They are part and parcel of travelling for females and most women are experienced in fending off or ignoring such mean gestures.

Another voice was also whispering in her head, however. Why must I put up with such petty insults because I am female? Why must my bus trip through the splendid countryside be spoiled? This clandestine attack was perpetrated with impunity on a stranger, a foreigner. In the close village community where this frustrated man comes from, he would never dare approach a woman thus.

During her deliberations the stiff arm continued to probe and his leg made more surreptitious forays toward her thigh. These were countered by hunching further into the corner. His breath was coming audibly now and uneven. He stared woodenly ahead, uninvolved in the passionate obsession of the rest of his body. His rigid, stiff face took no responsibility.

Thrusting aside, not only his advances, but also the casually liberated attitude ... Paula stood up. She squeezed past him and moved to the seat opposite.

There was someone already seated in the other half and Paula smiled apologetically for taking up the extra space. The response was a smile from her new seat companion. "Sit", she said.

One day we were fortunate enough to ride the Minotaur himself. When Paula's parents and sister were visiting we went one morning to the post office in Agios Mironas to change money. Linda elected to stay at home on her own. The post office was not very busy, the local priest was standing chatting with the clerk behind the desk. As he was counting out the drachma notes we heard a great roaring wind and the whole building shook. It lasted several seconds during which we were puzzled and took it to be an abrupt storm. During those few seconds, however, the post office clerk leapt up from his desk, scattering the money and flew out around us and out the door. Shortly after this the village priest gently but persistently took Allan, Paula's father, by the arm and propelled him outside too. We all followed. The roaring had stopped by this time but there was a stupendous commotion out on the street.

Everyone was screaming. "Seismos! (Earthquake!)" We were excited, this was our first earthquake but we were extremely disappointed that we hadn't even recognized it. The end was an anti-climax. No further tremors were felt and everyone slowly drifted back to their homes and shops. The clerk phoned home to ensure his family were safe, then relaxed, looking a little embarrassed. The priest laughed and joked with Allan and was thanked for his heroic attempt to save our lives.

We rushed home to see how Linda had fared. She had felt the tremor and had gone outside to open the gate and see what was happening in the lane. No one appeared to be too worried so she was not frightened; she thought it was rather fun. Michalis, who knew she was alone, came dashing across the street to see she was not hurt and to reassure her further, an act of great kindness for which we were very grateful.

Greece is currently undergoing one of its periodic cycles of frequent earthquake activity and more are anticipated everywhere. Earthquake drills are taught in every school and local phone books also carry two pages of instructions. A pamphlet enclosed with the electricity bill gave detailed instructions on how to earthquake-proof your home and what to do before, during and after a quake. After translating this booklet we moved two very large, glass covered prints from over our bed to the other side of the room.

We learned later that the magnitude of our earthquake was 6.1 but the epicentre was very deep below the Cretan Sea separating Crete and Santorini so very little damage was done. The most dangerous earthquakes are the shallow ones.

It is easy to see the connection which the Minoans made between the roaring bull and earthquakes. Having experienced an earthquake is to feel a sense of continuity with Minoan Crete, whose magnificent structures and entire culture were eventually destroyed by the raging underground deity personified by the bull. Now we have had our first earthquake, we feel we have truly arrived.

CHAPTER FOURTEEN

Exploring Crete

Scott Davies — FOURTEEN

Our village has proved to be an excellent centre for walking. There are literally dozens of farm roads, tracks, footpaths, etc., leading into the varied countryside right from our door. We take a walk on most days collecting horta, looking at wild flowers, birds, butterflies, etc. Our territory has now extended to cover Agia Varvara, Kroussonas and Agios Mironas, a radius of some 10 to 15 kilometres from the centre of Kato Asites. The countryside ranges from lush valleys to the low scrubland, called phrygana, and barren mountain tops.

We have explored some of the 3 200 caves in Crete, one of which is located in the mountain behind the village. Inside was evidence of human occupation, ashes from fires with sheep bones, broken pots, etc. This cave was used as a refuge for two British soldiers, names unknown, who remained in Crete after the evacuation of allied troops following the fall of Crete in 1941. After the evacuation there was a strong resistance movement involving allied soldiers and local Cretans which made the German occupation particularly difficult. These two soldiers blew up a German fuel dump in Dafnes, a village some 15 kms away. Despite the fierce retribution that this act brought down on the local population no one informed on them. This loyalty in the face of horrific pressure was typical of the behaviour of Cretans during these difficult times. We have been proudly shown a number of bullet holes in some of the houses and churches around the village.

There is another large cave system in the nearby gorge. This one has a lake which is said to feed an underground stream that comes out in a cave in Sarhos, some ten kilometres down the next valley. Some of the inner chambers of this cave contains hundreds of bats hanging from the roof. We have explored this cave system but have found no evidence of human occupation except for the entrance chamber which is still used as a shelter for the shepherd and his flock.

We have also walked in the higher mountains around our village, gradually going higher and farther from home as we have become more used to the terrain and the climate. Our first major expedition was to the mountain peak, apparently unnamed, immediately above the village. We set off upward via the sheep pasture where there is a fresh water spring and then continued up the south east ridge. After several hours and many false peaks leading to other ridges we arrived at the summit and were rewarded by magnificent views of the village and the higher peaks of the Psiloritis range. We made our descent down the north east ridge, to a road which seemed to lead back to the village. This was an illusion, we eventually had to cut across a precipitous, fallow field covered in prickly plants and find a very circuitous route back to the village via Gorgolaini. A long, hot, but enjoyable day.

Some months later we decided on a more challenging climb and set our sights on the highest mountain in our area, Koudouni. We packed the rucksack with fruit and chocolate and left the house early on a bright, clear morning, with the altimeter set at Kato Asites' altitude of 1 500 feet. We filled up our water flask at the sheep pens. A track from the pens met the marked route up to Prinos where there is a mountain refuge at 3 650 feet but we decided on a frontal assault on the mountain, by-passing the refuge.

The direct route was rough with lots of sharp stones and scree. The ascent required some exposed scrambling/climbing (hands, feet, hand-jams), for short sections, especially once Koudouni was reached. We arrived at the 6 100 feet (1 860 m) summit after four hours. There were majestic views of Crete's highest mountain, Psiloritis, covered in snow from November till August. We tried to return via another peak, Giristi, at 1 779 m but we managed to miss it and came down too far south and then had the tricky manoeuvre of contouring around loose scree slopes and gulleys to reach the track.

The approved track branches somewhere below the refuge and we missed the turn-off that leads to the sheep pen road. This meant that we ended up back on the long road that comes back to Kato Asites near Gorgolaini, the same road we ended up on when we climbed the other lower mountain in this area. Several of Crete's abundant birds of prey, including a buzzard and a Griffon vulture, were all we had for company. These slopes are also home to the rare lammergeyer, the largest bird of prey. This bird drops bones of carcasses from great heights to extract the marrow, hence its alternative name of Bonecrusher.

We have done much of our longer distance exploring in rental cars, often accompanied by visitors who happened to be staying with us. An old friend and drinking buddy, Dave, from Bristol fortuitously arrived during the Dafnes Wine Festival. After a day or so in Kato Asites for orientation and to adjust his palate to the local wine we set out for the festivities. On our way into Dafnes we passed two German tour buses parked on the side of the road, not a good omen. The village square was filled with tables and chairs, two long tables were occupied by the tour group. We selected an empty table and went in search of wine.

Seven large barrels were set up on one side of the square. On each of the barrels a large sign proclaimed the vineyard of origin. We went up to the counter with earthenware glasses and jugs and ordered half a kilo of retsina in our halting Greek. The response, in excellent English, was that all wine was free. We could buy or rent our glasses and jugs and help ourselves. Amazing! Food was available from the village hall, chicken, chops, salads and potatoes.

We bought our mugs and jug and settled down for the wine tasting, trying them all, retsina, white, rose (called red) and red (called black). In polite wine tasting circles it is usual to take a thimble-full, sip it carefully, swirl it around in the mouth and spit it out, with intermediate palate cleansing for each new wine. Our approach was to swig back a tumbler-full of each of the seven wines before deciding on one of the two non-resinated whites as our evening's tipple. By 10 pm every table was full with tourists and Greeks done up to the nines, including one lady with a spectacular, off-the-shoulder, gold dress with flounces, lace bows and sequins in most unlikely places.

When we had lost some of our inhibitions we approached the German table with a request for help with the translation of the directions from a package of prescription medicine. With great good will and much discussion they gave us an English rendering. (Later, we returned it to Eugenia, who then had to translate it again from English to Greek for her aunt.) Soon afterward, the dancing started and the whole crowd in the square joined in. Eating, drinking and general merriment continued into the early hours of the morning with our contingent doing at least our share of the drinking. We finally made our way home and had a last pre-bed beer as a cure for dehydration.

The next day was Sunday and we went for lunch in Kroussonos, about 8 miles around the mountain from our village. There were no tavernas or other sources of food open but we managed by eating the snacks served with the drinks, in one place it was melon and peanuts and in another fresh almonds. We then set off up the road to Agia Irini, a church and monastery above Kroussonos. Having got there we thought we might as well go a little farther up the mountain road to enjoy the views. The road was very rough and rutted but was reasonably flat for the first few kilometres. We consulted our far from accurate map which showed a single road going right over the mountain so we decided to continue a little farther. What our map didn't show was the many junctions with roads leading in all directions, all looking equally travelled. We found out that many of them lead 5-10 kilometres into the dead end of a sheep pasture. By the time we'd done several of these detours and had to retrace our steps we concluded that we were now probably over half way across. We had little choice but to continue. What we hadn't noticed till that moment was the fuel gauge, registering empty!

With a base of several retsinas on near-empty stomachs we

found this hilarious and drove merrily on. At an unexpectedly fertile plateau we saw a family having a meal break from tending their fruit trees. So there is life in them thar hills, we cried gaily to each other. They didn't look the type to rescue us with some of their petrol so we asked them instead whether we were on the right road for Anogia. They waved vaguely ahead and collectively gave us three widely different guesses at the distance. We continued, watching the potholes and the fuel gauge with equal lack of concern. One and a half hours after setting out from the monastery above Kroussonos for a short drive, we came miraculously to a paved road. This led downhill in sweeping curves and brought us, coasting but not yet completely dry according to the gas gauge, right into the first petrol station in Anogia. The petrol pump delivered slightly more than the capacity of the car's tank! Very few metres further on we stopped again to refill our own depleted liquid fuel tanks.

Anogia is a town renowned even among the mountain peoples for providing fierce resistance fighters against all invaders of Crete. During the German occupation in World War II this town and a number of surrounding villages were plundered, burned and then dynamited. All the men found were killed. This was officially an act of reprisal for the abduction of the German General Kreipe, some four months earlier, but another view is that it was an act intended to destroy any remaining resistance in the final months of the German occupation of Crete. The town today has a peculiar appearance that is at first difficult to pinpoint. Eventually it dawned on us that there is not a single old building. After the Germans left the entire town was rebuilt. We returned to

Kato Asites the long way round, via Heraklion, and arrived in time for a jolly session at Michalis' house.

The next day we left for an excursion on Crete's superhighway, the main Heraklion-Hania road, built by the Americans when they needed access to the naval base at Souda Bay. We lunched in Rethymnon, which has a picturesque old town little frequented by tourists and is home to the Humanities Faculties of the University of Crete. According to an old saying: "Hania for arms, Rethymnon for book-learning, Iraklion for drinking and Sitia for fornication". Unfortunately, we are not in a position to be able to confirm these descriptions from our studies of the various towns.

We made a leisurely detour to take a look at Crete's largest, and only permanent natural lake, lake Kournas at the village of Kavallos. Apart from a couple of tavernas, there isn't much there, although, with so little fresh water on the island Cretans are proud of this natural phenomenon.

Hania is an enchanting port town and former Venetian capital of Crete, with the old mosque now a tourist information cum ice cream shop. We stayed overnight in the historic Pension Teresa just off the port promenade. The suite was an old fashioned design, typical of Hania, with sleeping quarters perched above the room, accessed by a steep ladder.

After a cosmopolitan breakfast of fresh orange juice and real French croissants, we headed back towards Rethymnon for our return journey via the south coast. Leaving the main highway at Vrises and heading south up into the hills through beautiful country, we stopped at a shepherd's cottage. The cottage had been built there because of a deep well with abundant water, surprising at that altitude. With the new tourist boom, they had turned the shack into a two table rest stop. We were served by a shy mountain lad. We sat perched on the edge of a great cliff overlooking the White Mountains.

The road then led to Askifos, on the edge of a fertile plain with a Venetian fort. We drove on down through the magnificent scenery of the Imbros gorge heading towards the Minoan site of Phaistos, which was just shutting for the day at 7 pm. In the Phaistos car park we were approached by two young German women who were looking for a lift to the camp site at Matala. So we went to Matala. The south coast in this area is thick with back packers and campers, leftovers of the 1960's when Matala was a famous hippy hangout, hosting the likes of Bob Dylan, Joni Mitchell and Margaret Trudeau, the former wife of Canada's most famous prime minister. With some difficulty we managed to cram the tourists and their huge packs into our small Subaru and set off.

Matala is now a tired and jaded town of tavernas and rooms for rent, since living in the caves has been made illegal. The unlimited hospitality of the local residents was grossly abused by the hippies and flower children; residents are now quite properly cynical and sometimes distinctly unfriendly. If prices in the beachside tavernas are any indication, they are now getting their own back on the rich northerners.

Having a few drinks in a bar overlooking the beach we watched the fantastic sunset, improved by a power cut and candle-lit tables. On our way home we dined in Moires on a genuine, thin-crust wood oven pizza. The new pizza restaurant is run by a young local who returned to Moires after spending ten years working in restaurants in New York.

The next afternoon Michalis the Neighbour called, ostensibly to treat our grape vines for fungus with sulphur powder but really he was bored because Katerina had gone to her mother's house. We introduced him to gin and tonic which he found quite palatable. Michalis noticed that we were using oregano bought in a shop in Heraklion so arranged to take us herb picking the next morning. We had just finished clearing the table after Michalis left, chucking the remains of the snacks in the curry when Katerina arrived looking for Michalis, who had obviously left us to go to the cafenion. We started all over again, laid out fresh snacks and beers. Katerina loved the gin and tonic, it became a favourite with her.

Up early the next morning, we had a cup of tea and opened the gate to signal that we were ready, only to find the mechani already parked across the gate waiting for us. Michalis provided hats for those of us without them and we set off on the usual bone-shaking, breast-jiggling ride through the olive groves to the south west of the village. We parked not far out of town and followed Michalis through the groves until we were above the tree line. He explained to us that the best herbs were at the base of the cliffs high above.

We slogged on upwards getting hot and bothered even at that early hour. Once we reached the cliffs we started collecting oregano and aerondas, gradually moving upwards until we on the plateau at the cliff top. Aerondas is the local name for Dittany, Origanum dictamnus, a close relative of marjoram and oregano, although it looks quite different. It was a herb highly prized by the ancient Greeks for its healing qualities and is still commonly used today. Michalis strode off across the plain towards the base of the mountain where we eventually reached the shepherd's hut, belonging to Manolis the Butcher who has the shop next to Michalis' cafenion. Here we refreshed ourselves with the delicious, fresh cool water before heading off across the plain in the opposite direction from our arrival. We reached an overgrown track and soon descended back to the treeline and the olive groves. Michalis picked us some pears and sent us back to the mechani while he dashed off, sure-footed as a Cretan wild goat, for some more oregano.

We bumped our way back to Kato Asites and were invited to stay for some coffee, but were served raki and cakes, although it was now only 9.30 am. Next came some sliced cucumber. Just as we were going to leave, out came a large courgette omelette which was sliced up and offered around. Mike declined since he doesn't eat eggs, an excuse they surprisingly accepted. Dave and Paula ended up with loaded plates and wine was substituted for the raki. Mike declined any alternate food but soon ended up with a large plate of beans in sauce, which was then also served to Dave and Paula. We eventually staggered out at around 11 after they had given us a parting gift of two ornate and colourful backpacks, said to be 30 years old, made from woven lamb's wool.

Once we had recovered, Dave helped with some plumbing jobs, including relocating our yard tap and inserting a non-return valve in the water supply. Due to our earlier oversight in this crucial detail we had been draining our water tank back into the city mains whenever the supply was interrupted.

With other visitors we have extensively explored most of the south coast. One of our favourite areas is near Preveli Monastery. Hopelessly lost on our first trip, as only experienced map readers can be in Crete, we ended up in spite of ourselves, at the coastal village of Damnoni. We were looking for a place to stay but at first glance it seemed a village composed only of tavernas. We had lunch instead, at a taverna by the sea watching a woman at the next table mixing oil and vinegar, to make French dressing, in the ashtray. Her husband made no comment so we assumed it must be a curious family custom. "Peter, be a dear and call the waiter to bring us an ashtray so I can eat my salad." We were rather hoping they were smokers, to see what would happen next.

After lunch we followed a coast road that wasn't marked on the map and after bottoming out only twice we arrived at a beach with sand of one of the most rare and exquisite consistencies we have ever encountered in a career of many years spent on warm coastal fringes. Amoudi Beach is neither sand nor stone, but pebbles so tiny they massage, rather than gouge your bare feet as you walk on it. You could lay in it, soaking wet after a swim, and get up and brush the tiny pebbles off your body with the most desultory flick of the wrist. This area of the coast also has some of the best snorkelling in Crete with fresh, plump sea-urchins just waiting to be gathered up, split open, doused in lemon juice and swallowed!

Best of all there was an hotel, set back a few hundred metres from the beach and only a very few caravans parked under the tamarisk trees at the back of the beach. They were presumably attracted there by the fresh water hose left permanently flowing into the sand from the stream emptying out onto the beach and which was a huge attraction with children under 60. We booked into the hotel and drove off again to another spot on the map for dinner.

We never found the spot on the map but we did find a long precipitous road back down to the coast and after driving for about 40 kilometres we ended up at another taverna perched above a beach almost within site of our hotel. To get to this spot you pass the Skinaria Beach Hotel, which all our guidebooks priced and rated, in spite of the fact that it has never opened since its completion 5 years ago, owing to some error in compliance with regulations or some failure to find a sympathetic friend in the right Government department. Nor, despite its name, is it near the beach.

The taverna has a breathtaking view of the small cove, stream, sand beach and Libyan Sea. We hardly noticed it. Our entire party of six was riveted by the sight in the immediate foreground below the restaurant - a man engaged in his extensive, detailed, thorough and fastidious toilette beside his motorbike. He washed, nay he bathed. He shaved. He trimmed. He anointed. He combed.

We watched. And, of course, we speculated. He was young, tall, well-muscled, red-headed, with a slight tan. It was a 4 to 2 vote for British over American for his nationality. On reflection, he probably heard every word of our conversation as our voices wafted downward from the open terrace. To our great delight he seemed to be coming to dine at our taverna. Not surprising, since there was no other.

"Ask him where he comes from," hissed the 15 year old of our party as he came up the steps. But he beat us to it.

"Can you recommend anything on the menu?" he asked in a Manchester accent, as if we were intimate acquaintances (which we probably were by now). "Where are you from?"

Got us!

Some months later, once most of the tourists had left the island, we decided to rent a car and explore more of Crete on our own, without the excuse of showing visitors around. We set out on a partly cloudy November morning, passing a fishmonger in Prinias village square choosing fish for a housewife as two cats sat hopefully underneath. There was a flock of sheep waiting to cross the road near Agia Varvara. A sheepdog held them back until the traffic had passed.

We turned towards Gangales just before Agia Deka to drive through the Messara Plain, the most fertile region of Crete. It supplies Crete and Greece with vegetables, much of them grown under very ugly and untidy looking plastic greenhouses. During gale force winds the plastic is ripped off the frames and scattered around the south coast, greatly detracting from the attractiveness of the coastal areas. At that time of year the plain looked much drier than our area, which has been trapping the mountain rains. The dry bed of the Geropotamus river, one of Crete's rare rivers, ran between us and the Kofinas Mountains to the South. Olive trees were heavily laden with green berries weighing the branches down. The farmers must be more prosperous here, they drive tractors instead of mechanis.

It was market day in Pirgos and we became caught in the traffic, mostly pedestrian, although a truck was stopped in the middle of the road while the driver chatted with a stall owner. One black face, a man selling music tapes reminded us that in bygone days Crete and Africa were major trading partners.

Later on we picked up a woman going from Tertsa to Sikilogos with vegetables for market. As we drove along chatting she kept taking out more and more produce from her bag. She showered us with aubergines and peppers. Had she been going much further, or needed many more rides she would have arrived at the market empty handed, such was her generosity. In Ierapetra we managed to find the only open taverna that didn't have any food. The taverna owner said that everything had been eaten the night before and his wife was busy cooking more cheese pies, etc.

We arrived in Palekastro by early evening and stayed at the Hotel Helas, which was the only one open. The next morning in the local cafenion we were charged 150 Drx each for coffee for which everyone else was being charged 100 Drx. Also we did not get the usual glass of water with it, although all the locals did. End of season fatigue was setting in in tourist country.

Roussolakos archaeological site is being restored, with evidence of recent excavations. It was deserted at that time of year, however, and we were free to wander around undisturbed. Apparently a town, with ordinary houses, this site has given archaeologists insight into daily life in Minoan times.

Arriving at the Kato Zakros palace archaeological site we found that it was still open, with an attendant at the kiosk but was nearly deserted, with a small handful of late tourists. The site in winter is partly submerged and the seaward fringes of it were already underwater with the recent rains. The drowned location does not reflect the bad planning of Minoan architects, but has been caused by the slow sinking of the east end of the island. The harbour for Zakros, if it still exists, is fully submerged. It is yet to be discovered.

The guidebooks do not describe half the site, which contains a large number of houses and/or outbuildings, but the excavator, Dr. Nicholas Platon, has written a book about the site. It gives a clear and fascinating account of the excavation of the site and a description of its magnificent finds. It is unique among Minoan sites in having been completely abandoned during its destruction in the Thera volcanic eruption and subsequent earthquakes and fires. Consequently there has been a large number of extremely important finds. Zakros is also unique among Minoan palaces in containing evidence of kitchen facilities! The inhabitants were apparently frantically trying to propitiate the underworld gods or goddesses during the destruction. Included among the offerings were small pieces of pumice from the explosion of the Thera volcano.

There was an end of season feel in the tavernas on the sea front but we managed to get a cold drink at the last open taverna. If we had come one day later, all would have been shut for the season.

Unfortunately, the track to Xerocambos was closed so instead of completing a circuit to the south coast road, we took the very poor mountain track from Andravasti to Karidi and Sitamos. The landscape is covered with a beautiful violet coloured soil, interspersed with large jagged boulders and bright purple heather. We met only one shepherd along the route and numerous musical flocks of sheep and goats grazing the prickly vegetation. To our surprise, after Katsidoni the road was paved, although it is marked on the map as a dirt track. The 30 km journey from Andravasti to Piskokephalo took two hours. Maps are deliberately misleading and inaccurate in Greece, direction-finding is a military secret here.

We had lunch in an almost deserted Sitia and took the north road west. A branch near Messa Mouliana leads to the beautiful isolated village of Kalavros, perched on a narrow clifftop 200 metres above the sea, with spectacular views of the rocky coastline, but with no apparent route down to the water. We wondered what the villagers do for a living. Surely, they could not be fishermen, although only a short distance from the sea. There were small olive groves scattered on the few hillside slopes which were not too steep.

Nearby Mochlos is in a completely different setting, nestled on the sea along a narrow low coast. It has been recently "discovered" and has a new huge hotel complex near the village. The village itself, which is used by American archaeologists excavating the nearby island, is still picturesque. The new tarmac road to the village will ensure, however, that it won't long remain that way.

We returned to Sitia and Zakros again a few months later armed with Platon's book on the site and accompanied by an archaeologist friend, Val Ward from South Africa.

We left Mike at the top of the gorge and he walked down the Valley of the Dead to Kato Zakros. The steep sides of the gorge are studded with caves and chambers that were used by Minoans as burial chambers although only one body was found there during modern excavations. It is a beautifully tranquil walk, accompanied only by birds and butterflies grazing on the oleanders and wild flowers. The gorge ends at the sea and the Kato Zakros archaeological site.

The Kato Zakros site is one of the most accessible to the imagination but it's location at the bottom of a townsite and the finds in the "palace" are convincing evidence that archaeologists since Arthur Evans have misinterpreted the nature of these structures. Their purpose was much more likely to have been religious and community oriented than a mere royal residence. No remains have ever been be found that could be remotely described as bedroom furniture or accoutrements in the "king's megaron" or "queen's megaron" in any of Crete's palaces. Indeed, the queen's megaron is always arbitrarily selected as the smaller and less stately of the two. Furthermore, a king's palace seems hardly credible when there is not a shred of incontrovertible evidence for any kings anywhere in Minoan Crete, in the modern sense of supreme monarch. Platon justifies his description of the eastern wing as the "residential quarters" by their similarity to the "residential quarters" at Knossos. The Knossos bedrooms were designated as such by Evans before he had even excavated them!

Rodney Castleden, in his highly sensible book, "Minoans, Life in Bronze Age Crete", seems to have looked at the problem with considerably more objectivity than Evans, who was fettered by his Victorian sense of world order. Castleden argues convincingly that the "palaces" are religious structures or temples, analogous with many other sites in the areas of the ancient world where the Cretans are thought to have originated. All the imposing structures in Egypt and the Middle East have religious origins. In the Bronze Age religion played a central role in the lives of all people. In addition, since almost all Minoan frescoes and sealstones show women, not men, in positions of authority, it seems unlikely that the ruler would have been male, if there were only one. Clearly there is a need for more female archaeologists, who might be less inclined to assume that a patriarchal figure must be sought in all civilizations.

The role of women in Minoan society is crystal clear on the frescoes and sealstones and carvings. Who is sitting front row centre at the theatre? To whom is the cup-bearer carrying his offering in the great Processional Fresco at Knossos? Who is standing with lionesses at her feet and the Horns of Consecration behind her? Who is represented in ivory, gold, faience and all the other precious materials of the day? It certainly is NOT King Minos! Male figureheads are almost certainly a later corruption by the degenerate Myceneans who invaded Crete and took advantage of her misfortunes after the great eruptions and earthquakes.

Still musing on Minoans, we drove back through the village of Ano Zakros and passed an open lorry selling baby chicks. Most households keep chickens for eggs and stewing hens and itinerant chick sellers are a common sight. It was not so common, however, to find chicks scattered about on the road in the middle of nowhere. Two forlorn looking babies were rather shaken from their fall off the back of the lorry and were looking for water and shelter, in great danger of becoming pressed chicken by the oncoming traffic. In an ill-considered act of charity, Mike screeched the car to a halt. We rounded them up and put them in the hatchback just behind Val, where she spent the rest of the journey back to the Knossos Pizzeria and Rooms in Palekastro cooing at them. We found an old water bottle and some grass to keep them happy while we had lunch and then asked Giorgos at the hotel for a box to transport them back to Kato Asites the next day.

Mike wanted straightaway to give the chicks names, although he also pretended that we should give them to Giorgos. It seemed appropriate to name them after our two visitors (Mike's brother Dave was also with us but would rather fry on a beach than fry among Minoan ruins.) Since Val was in on the find she got first choice of names and chose, of course, the black one, since she is African.

They spent the night in our hotel room. They slept and we didn't. They needed the rest in order to serenade us at full volume all the way back home. Val felt sorry for them and tucked them under her wing where they rewarded her by pooping all over her nice t-shirt.

We made a cosy little home for them in our avli where they provided constant entertainment. The two chicks gained 100 g a week for several weeks and slowly took on adult plumage and characteristics. After 4 weeks it became clear they were aptly named when our neighbour Maria the Cheekpincher informed us that Dave wouldn't be providing us with eggs. "Never mind," she said, "he can't make eggs, but he can make soup."

The local children were amused for several days after they spotted our unique method of proffering delicacies to the chickens. All available fly swatters in the neighbourhood were requisitioned to provide a steady supply of squished bugs. Soon the slap of the swatter was enough to bring both chicks running. Many of our neighbours stopped by to peer in at the chickens and comment on their increasing size. You would have thought they had never seen chickens before, although every household in the village has at least half a dozen. They thought it hilarious that we had given them names, but very shocked that we had named them after our friends. "Does Valerie know?", they worried.

When we started putting toys in the chicken coop they were certain we were completely deranged. Some wind chimes provided audio stimulation. A mirror gave Dave endless occupation, challenging the newcomer on the roost; Valerie was not vain and barely gave herself a glance. A sandbox was a nice cool spot to scratch in on hot days. One day we had our English neighbour from Nisi for lunch and she brought the chickens a small green ball, suggesting we teach them to play football. Before we had the opportunity to develop the new sport, however, a small boy from the village spotted the ball. He sidled up to the chicken coop and when he thought we weren't looking, lifted it neatly and ran out of the gate with it.

When Val (the chick) became ill a constant stream of bedside visitors dropped in hourly to assist in diagnosis and suggest home remedies. The consensus was that she had over-eaten and Ritsa solemnly suggested that we operate, empty her stomach contents and sew her up again. Fortunately, she recovered in spite of our tender ministrations, which included Ritsa prodding her with a stick to get her out of her sheltered hidey hole for another round of examination. They were finally donated to an unknown recipient via Aristea's the Shop good offices when we had to leave on a business trip.

CHAPTER FIFTEEN

Settling In

We have now had our house for more than five years. However, due to other commitments and the need for major reconstruction work before it was habitable we have only managed to spend a total of some twenty four months here. This intermittent residency has meant that our Greek has suffered many setbacks while we have been away in other parts of the world and we have had to start almost from scratch on our returns to the village. More recently we have managed to curtail our travelling and are able to spend relatively long periods at home.

Our Greek has progressed to the extent that we are now able to hold some reasonable conversations with people. We are also beginning to be treated as locals with some people becoming closer to us and others drifting away to some extent as the novelty of our foreignness wears off and we are seen as just other residents of the village. We are now given fewer gifts of food, olive oil, lacework, etc., than we were in the early days but are treated more like members of the community. This means that we still get very willing help to solve any problems we might have but as part of a two-way process between equals. Our visitors, however, are still given the treatment afforded to strange and exotic foreigners and receive the full blast of "philokseni" (hospitality to strangers) with gifts and questioning from most people they meet. We are now in a better position to assist them with translation and to suggest suitable answers to some of the more personal questions.

One of the families who have drifted away is our close neighbours, Michalis and Katerina. We must have offended them in some way we were unable to identify and therefore powerless to rectify. In the past they had been very friendly, with occasional bouts of coolness when they did not visit so frequently, which we came to accept as normal. Then, over a short period we noticed that their greetings became positively brusque and were avoided altogether if they could possibly pretend they hadn't seen us. We were enormously saddened by this change as we had grown extremely fond of this family and counted them among our best friends and the most pleasant to socialize with in the village. Invitations to visit us were refused and after a couple of unequivocal snubs we retreated to lick our wounds and made no further overtures.

We spent hours discussing what we could have done and how we might make up the unknown transgression. We became very depressed. We invented increasingly elaborate theories involving a variety of causes, in some of which we were arch villains and in others were innocent bystanders to internal family problems. In one sense the predicament demonstrated a new maturity in our relationships in the village. While newcomers, we were treated to the universal "philokseni" for which Cretans are renowned. Now, however, we were becoming real individuals. It is inevitable that our personalities will not suit everyone and hence, as we became better known, we became less well liked. Not an exceptionally cheerful thought and we hoped it would not become generally true!

We contemplated a full frontal approach in asking what we had done and how to make good our error, hoping to make them understand that any affront could only have been caused by cultural ignorance and not by deliberate insult. We abandoned this approach as far too delicate for our clumsy vocabulary. In the meantime, we were as courteous as we were able when we did meet and hoped for better days eventually. We were disheartened by the thought of living in isolation in the midst of the village, ostracized by the locals.

During this period, we began to cherish the regular visits by several village children, aged about 5 to 16, who dropped in frequently for a drink or chat and to play with our exotic household accoutrements, especially a rotating office chair. One evening we were invited by Ritsa to her parents house for coffee at 8 pm. At the appointed time, however, there was complete silence at her house. We sat miserably with our gifts in the courtyard with the open gate, uncertain whether to storm in anyway or wait for Ritsa to fetch us. We thought perhaps the invitation had been issued without the knowledge of her frenzied Mum who was always busy caring for seven children. We didn't want to intrude at a bad time and disrupt her schedule.

At 8:05 we peaked out the gate and gazed at the unusually deserted street. At 8:15 we theorized that it was so quiet they must be all inside eating and perhaps cursing us for being late. At 8:20 we went up to our balcony and peered over into their deserted courtyard. At 8:30 we went up again and saw one of the sons chatting to his friend. A polite hello was issued from our balcony but not taken up. Then at nine o'clock Ritsa bounced into the yard and announced they had been to a nearby village on a visit, which made it clear that the invitation, though genuine, was unexpected by the rest of the family. She sat a minute, said, "Just a sec" and went off home not to be seen again that evening. We assumed she had gone to ask permission from Mum for our visit and been told it wasn't a good time. We were grateful we hadn't blundered in.

This kind of sitting uncertainly in limbo has been a major feature of our socializing in Crete. Because invitations are issued so frequently and so casually we are never sure whether we are truly expected on any specific occasion. Trusting to the fact that if the invitation is serious we will be fetched or phoned at the appropriate hour, we linger in uncertainty, sometimes for hours. Similarly, when we invite friends we are never absolutely sure that they will show up and if they do, when. We wait anxiously with food overcooking and the bread going stale. Sometimes they arrive just as we have decided to trail miserably off to bed. Then disappointment and an early night are transformed into a heightened party atmosphere, with laughter and wine and, always, too much food.

After being rebuffed by our friends the wait in the courtyard for Ritsa was acutely agonizing to our sensitized minds. The next day, however, we learned there were exceptional circumstances that night. Ritsa's 91 year old grandmother died in hospital. We heard the toll for the dead but didn't know who it was until we went to mine our unending source of information, Aristea the Shop. All that day people we rarely see in our neighbourhood trooped by in dark clothes to pay their respects to the body, which had been brought home for burial.

Many of them stopped by for a cool drink and some melon. First three aging men we often see in the cafenion dropped in to see our house. Then Aristea the Shop brought Amalia the Cafenion, who hadn't yet been for a visit, although her kids had. Lonely old Yannis the Widower also stopped in.

After the funeral in the late afternoon more people came by. Michalis the Cafenion must have had reports from his wife; he came with the excuse of delivering a letter and found his daughter with us together with Melanthia, only daughter of our other neighbours, Yannis the Bulldozer and Argiro. We switched from orange drinks to beer and wine and brought out snacks. The house began to take on a festive atmosphere, albeit subdued, and we could feel our depressions lifting. From believing yesterday that the whole village had gone off us, here we were, breaking all previous records for hospitality. Even our aloof ex-friend Michalis couldn't control his curiosity and came by to join the party. Twice! It was just like the good old days when we were bosom buddies. Life in Crete was suddenly great again and all well with our world.

In order to minimize the chance of offending the villagers, one of our early concessions to possible sensitivities was never to appear in the village in shorts since we had never seen any but the very young dressed in this way. However, most of our work on the house in the summer has been carried out wearing the minimum amount of clothing consistent with comfort and modesty. Consequently we change into long trousers whenever we go beyond our gate out into the village, although we have been assured by many that it is unnecessary. The one time Paula did wear knee length shorts on our way to the beach she got laughed at good-naturedly by Aristea the Shop.

One early habit that we have outgrown was never to face the village alone. People in the village used to comment on the fact that we were inseparable, little knowing that we were terrified of the strangeness and needed each other's presence to bolster our courage. There was also the very practical advantage of two heads being better than one when it came to communication. We now blithely step out alone whenever we feel like it, secure in the knowledge that we are now amongst friends that we can communicate with.

A similar change has occurred with the street gate issue. Opening it used to be a major occasion, and trial, in our early days here. Now, if we feel like being sociable we leave the gate open and will exchange greetings with passers by or receive more extended visits from some of our friends. Usually such visits are occasions for a cold drink or a coffee together with a snack ranging from nuts or fruit to a sample of whatever we happen to be cooking. Other occasions turn into a full-blown session with ouzo, beer, wine and a multi-course meal. In either case we are now comfortable with the sheer informality and friendliness of our neighbours and have largely learned to abandon our former inhibited ways of formal dinner invitations and set time-tables for social affairs. It's all much more relaxed and pleasant, although we still can't match the average village housewife's skill of being able to offer a feast to any visitor (or even crowd of visitors) who happen to arrive unannounced.

We have become unofficial English tutors for all the local kids who have trouble with their homework. Having volunteered to help several of our neighbours, we are now seen as a resource for any student in difficulties. Some of the English lessons of the Cambridge Higher Certificate are extremely obscure. How do you use "voice stress analyzer" in a sentence? one girl wanted to know. Where on earth do they get this stuff? We enjoy this volunteer work very much, it is one of the ways we can contribute significantly to village life. We are occasionally given oil or a plate of food by the student's mother and in this way we have become part of the normal exchange system on which the village operates.

Another of our contributions to the community is as resident experts on all sorts of construction/plumbing/electrical problems and a source of free tool rental. In these ways our life here is no longer a one way street of kindness and we feel much more comfortable about being part of the community. We now pay local taxes on our electricity, phone and water bills. We contribute donations to the local schools during their fund-raising drives and shop in the local shops. We have a much better idea of how the village runs and of the local politics. As we walk down the main street, people greet us by name and invite us to sit for a coffee in their homes or in the cafenia. Although this was very hard work initially we now enjoy these encounters, using them, as the locals do, to find out the latest gossip and village news. When we were unfamiliar with the village we almost always refused these invitations, especially from women, who seem to have a great deal of work to do. Recently, we were taken to task for these refusals by a friend.

"Why don't you ever sit with Argiro?", Yannis asked us. "When I am out all day she is bored and lonely. You are busy, you say, you have too much work to do. What work? Come. Come for coffee."

In truth, we claimed to have work in order not to bother Argiro in HER work, but we see now that she really would like us to visit. The very next day we spent an hour with her and were able to solve a problem she was having with her camera.

The restoration work on the house is largely completed and it is a comfortable place to live. Cool in summer and warm in winter with our wood stove set up in the living room. It has lived up to our hopes and expectations. As one of our Greek visitors said, the house does have a nice friendly feel to it. Long may it continue.

We have managed to maintain most of the attractive appearance of the buildings and, in many cases improve it, such as by exposing stonework that had been plastered over. The locals seem impressed by what we have done although they probably would have done it differently themselves. For example, they all seem to like super-smooth plastered walls and don't understand our preference for a more undulating appearance. They do appreciate some of our modern appliances, particularly the ceiling fans and the washing machine. They also all admire the ceramic tiled floors that we have laid throughout the house. The tasks left now are more in the line of on-going maintenance of what is still a very ancient structure despite all our innovations and improvements.

Our over-confidence came back to bite us when we returned to Kato Asites, after a recent overseas trip. We took a late night charter from the UK arriving in Heraklion at around 3 am, tumbled into a taxi and said "take us home". On the way we talked about how relaxed we now were about arriving at the house after an absence, compared with our early dread of the latest catastrophes that would await us. Passing through Agios Mironas the taxi had to thread its way through tables, chairs and the remnants of the revellers who were still celebrating the saint's day at nearly 5 am.

We paid off the taxi and carried our bags into the house to be met by an appalling stench. It was coming from the fridge which obviously had been without electricity for a considerable time. A check of the supply system showed that someone had turned off the main supply to our house, a simple procedure since the main isolation switch is part of the meter and is readily accessible in the street outside. We learned that this is a favourite sport amongst the village lads and is usually just a minor inconvenience. In this case it had been a bit more serious. Apart from the spoiled food and the stinky fridge it also meant that we had been without our fax and answering machine, a disaster when trying to run an international company.

A closer look around the house revealed water damage in two of the rooms, hard to understand in the height of the dry summer. Discussion in the village the next day confirmed that we had had a very heavy downpour about a week after we had left, absolutely unprecedented in August. This driving rain had poured in through two of the doors that we would normally have sealed had we left in winter. So much for our confidence, the village and the house can still provide some surprises.

Still, to look on the bright side, the heavy rain did mean that most of our plants survived and the grape vines growing over our crevatina looked full of vigour reaching out to provide shade on our balcony.

The children of the taverna family are growing up. Recently we had an odd conversation with Manolis and Maria at the taverna about the children and about life. The place was deserted. It was the day after Yannis' name day and it was as quiet as a tomb. The night had been hectic: gunshots echoing from all over the village, music, voices, laughter, shouting until dawn. People partying, celebrating, dancing, tearing around in cars and motorcycles. The next day people were in their homes, sleeping it off, cleaning the house, regrouping. Lethargy oozed into the cafenia, men barely keeping up desultory conversations. Some frankly sleeping, their chairs propped against the wall.

Eugenia didn't come down from upstairs because she wasn't feeling well, so we chatted with Manolis. As we entered he wasn't in his usual spot in front of the TV. He was standing on the stage, trying to fix something with the window where the rain and wind were coming in. It had been raining non-stop for over a week and the weather was getting everyone down. Nonetheless, Manolis, as usual, was friendly, but perhaps a little weary too. He set the mood when Kostas came in. Instead of "hello", he had asked by way of greeting, "is it still raining?" He had asked us the same as we entered the doorway. "Good rain", he had called it. "For heaven's sake, haven't we had enough?", we asked. "It's been raining steadily for more than a week." "It is a long dry summer", he replied, " we need it". Then he sat at our table and gave Kostas instructions. Kostas was now old enough to begin learning the trade. First the obvious, lay the plastic table cloth and prepare for the meal. Then, unexpectedly, wistfully, an imaginary order as if he were a customer sitting with us. He ordered all his favourite foods, broad beans, salad and shrimps. "Bring wine", he said and then remembered he was out of stock. "Bring retsina. I'll go get some more wine tomorrow", he promised, forcing himself back to reality.

After she had made her ten thousandth cabbage salad and the millionth hand-cut chip Maria settled down to her needlework by the wood stove near us. Tonight she was sewing together fragments of a large tablecloth of complex design crocheted by her mother. Eugenia's dowry. A remnant of the old-fashioned values and traditional ways and perhaps the entree into the discussion which followed. She expressed her satisfaction with the rain. It meant she had another day's reprieve from the tyranny of olive picking and could stay home. Maria is sick of picking olives. She is a heavy woman and suffers from phlebitis; in fact she has an antipathy to movement and exercise of almost any kind. More than that, though she is just plain bored with the routine of repetitious agricultural chores. Manolis then said that he and Kostas had been out to spread fertilizer under the vineyards and olive groves. Maria giggled a little maliciously, gloating that in two or three days, when the olives were finished she was off-duty as far as outdoor work was concerned. "I'm finished, through, all done outside."

On the other hand, said Manolis, he had to start soon on trimming the grapes. He sounded fed up and we asked, "was he tired of being a farmer, didn't he like the work?"

"It's good work," he said, not very convincingly. Philosophically, he praised the abstract joys of farming and then, surprisingly, talked about turning the taverna into a supermarket, perhaps for Kostas to run. Maria and Manolis are thinking now about settling their children. They are comparatively wealthy and the children will be comfortably provided for.

Eugenia, they said would soon get married, next year, or the next, although she is only 19 and has no particular boyfriend. In fact, she had ambitions to become an English teacher, then to work in the tourist industry but both these schemes fell through, partly because her conservative parents are not very keen to see her go away to school. She hates farming and dreams about having exciting work in a glamorous office. Dreams, but she somehow never quite manages to take any initiatives which would be a step toward getting her out of the village. In a short time she probably will be married, and shortly after that will be a village housewife with kids, just like her mother.

Her dad will be happy when she is married, in the care of a good man, nearby. Her mother, however, looks a little bit doubtful. She herself has a good, hardworking, faithful, devoted husband. They are not poor. They have two polite, loving, well-behaved children. She has no reason to complain. And yet, once we asked Maria if she is happy and she said, softly, "no". Her life is circumscribed by the walls of her house, cooking, cleaning, serving. She doesn't even get to talk to the customers in the taverna. It is not respectable for women to serve at table in traditional tavernas. They are supposed to stay in the kitchen, safe from ... what? Temptation? Knowledge? Excitement? Maria never goes anywhere or does anything for her own pleasure. She feels caught in the timeless, joyless grind of the Cretan housewife.

Manolis has no such qualms. Although he loves Eugenia very much he is a conservative man and can not envisage a better fate for her than to remain within the security and protection of her family and their way of life.

Women in Crete like Maria found their fate more bearable until they began to get glimpses of the world outside, where women travel, have jobs, seem to be having a good time. Free. And seeing the life she missed, Maria is not at all certain that her life will be good for Eugenia. Safe, certainly. And predictable. But boring and unfulfilling. It is more difficult to see the disadvantages of modern living from their distance.

The latest big news in the village is the opening of a souvlaki shop. It opened in the old abandoned cafenion which used to belong to Stavros the Welder's father. They say years ago that it was the liveliest cafenion in the village. After Stavros' father died the cafenion closed and the building languished. Ever since we've been in the village it has been deserted and we have often peeked through the broken windows at the enormous old wine barrel in the corner and a long carved settle along the wall.

About three months ago Stavros rented it to a man from the village, Nikos, and his brother-in-law from Thessaloniki, Christos, who is reputed to know about gyros and souvlaki - he had a shop up north on the mainland. They renovated, plastered and painted inside and out. We thought our luck was in when they pulled out an old lintel we were hoping to beg for our outdoor oven. It was just 7 cm too short though. The wine barrel disappeared, we heard Stavros took it to his house. Alas, the lovely old settle was chopped up for firewood.

On opening night everyone in the village turned out. When you walked down the street you could hear the kids calling out to each other, younger ones tugging their parents along, "Come on Kosti, we're goin' to the souvlaki shop". Niko's Mum invited us to drink a krasaki (winette) but when we went we couldn't get near the place for people.

We waited a decorous three days for the first crush to dissipate. We couldn't wait any longer because Aristea kept asking us if we'd been yet and anyway our curiosity couldn't keep us away. When we were there the first time we sat down and had a gyro plate and souvlaki plate, to test the mettle of the joint. Wine was on the house for our first visit. There was a bit of trouble with the gyro machine, which provided discreet entertainment. They couldn't keep it lit, which gave us a moment's twinge about bacteria and trichinosis. The stand-by gas bottle was called into play and after several more attempts the thing was finally operational. Subdued cheers from the kitchen mingled with embarrassment in case anyone had noticed the teething troubles.

Shortly after Papa Yannis arrived, appearing majestically and filling the entire doorway, with "Good Health and God bless". He was treated to a soft drink and gyro and while he waited he made a royal tour of the few tables crammed into the room.

Several people dropped by to lend a hand with the new shop and our order was taken two or three times, which helped in almost getting it right and we had two offers of bread and napkins. Nikos' son stopped clearing the plates to have a chat with us about seeing us high up on the mountain. "Don't you remember me", he said to Paula, "I'm the one with the dog who jumped up and got your clothes all muddy."

Kids have adopted the souvlaki shop as an alternative hangout to the cafeteria. Early in the evening mums with their kids come in for a gyro-pitta (only 300 Drx, a meal in itself with sliced pork, tomatoes, onions, tsatsiki and chips, all rolled into a pitta bread). THE way to have it is "Ap ola", or "loaded". Older folks come later. It doesn't seem to close down till the rack of gyros is finished and all the village is asleep.

Our first visit was so much fun that we stopped in again the next night for a take-away gyro on the way home from a raki making party. We had just nipped down to the cafenion before dinner to see if we had any mail. Just as we entered Michalis the Cafenion came in carrying two plastic jerry cans. He was on his way to make raki from the grapes we had watched him stomp a month previously. We followed him and his two cans through the moonless night down dark alleys and fields to the still. It looked like a scene from Hades, with the large wood fire and copper-bellied stove billowing steam and smoke. Almost his whole family was seated on a long wooden plank set on bricks near a table full of barbecued pork chops and baked potatoes, cooked on embers dragged straight out of the fire. Grandpa was having trouble keeping the youngest out of his way when he was trying to stoke the fire and out of the raki which was pouring warm and fiery straight from the cooling coils. The little dear kept sticking her fingers into the stream and licking them, getting more and more boisterous and unmanageable. By the way, this time we had film in the camera.

And so it continues. We are now getting a feel for the natural rhythms and cycles of village life. We too now look forward to particular times or events that we had at first found alien and confusing. We still feel the magic of Crete. It may not be Eden but it's close enough for us.

APPENDIX ONE

Seasons

January

Olive picking is at its height, a distinctly uncomfortable task during this cold, wet season, the wettest month of the year. The olive oil factory sometimes works through the night. Many groves are sprayed with weed killer around this time to rid them of the abundant growth of wild plants which make finding the olives more difficult.

The first cherry and almond blossoms and wild narcissi appear on the hillsides to give hope for the coming of the spring. Yellow hillsides are formed by the clover-like *Oxalis* and by mustard plants.

In season: Apples, oranges, mandarins, all the leafy vegetables such as lettuce and cabbage, beets, dill, leeks, horta which is now picked in abundance on the hillsides and in fields.

February

Farmers are planting new grapes and olives, trimming and tying grape vines to the supports. Olive picking continues, as does weed killing.

Wildflowers appear abundantly among the *Oxalis* and other green growth as the days lengthen. Dominant wildflowers are the yellow peas *(Vicia)* and *Brassica nigra* as well as other species of mustard, purple and red varieties of *Anemone coronaria.* Purple irises *(Iris inguicularis)*, rosemary, mandrakes, *Euphorbia* and wild almonds are in flower.

In season: Oranges at their peak, apples, bananas, maratha (wild fennel) as well as leeks and other horta, dill, celery, courgettes.

March

Farmers rototill their fields,(mainly their vineyards) many looking exhausted after the day's work with the heavy vibrating two-stroke machines which bounce dangerously on rocks. Grape vines have now all been trimmed and new growth is just starting. It is a daily task to tie the tender shoots to the supporting wires. Lagana bread marks the first day of Lent; halva and dried beans being sold for the lenten season. Olives are mostly finished and trees are trimmed for the year.

A large number and great variety of spring flowers appear, including more irises and tulips, borage, giant orchids, the white, daisy-like, *Anthemis chia* and *Anemone heldreichii*, sweet peas, *Euphorbia characias*, cyclamens, asphodel and *Eruca*. Whole fields are bright yellow with vrouves and *Oxalis*. Chrysanthemums start blooming at the end of the month. Wild almonds and rosemary still in flower. Many butterflies, particularly peacocks, cabbage whites and fritillaries flock to the blossoms.

In season: A riot of Lenten vegetables, huge red radish, white radish, aubergine, early artichokes from warmer parts of Crete, oranges, dill, carrots, fresh koukia (broad beans) in their pods. Wild leeks are now old and tough but horta still abundant and eaten daily.

April

Early in the month the first trickle of tourists begin to pass through Kato Asites. Summer always starts on April 20th (says Nikos the Shop), up until that date there might still be cold weather and/or rain. Wood stoves are dismantled around the village.

Flowers are starting to form on the olive trees. Chrysanthemums, hyacinths, broom and all yellow March flowers. Pink and violet flowers begin to make an appearance, including sage. Almonds form fruit on the trees in the countryside. Plum trees have green fruit. Late in April, the fruit are forming on the wild fig trees. More butterflies, including the very common Scarce Swallowtail. Return of the swifts, Cretan weasels become active. Lots of hawks around.

In season: Strawberries from Messara, lettuce. Cabbages have disappeared.

May

This is sheep shearing month for the shepherds, the hardest time of the year. Farmers are still tying up grapes and clearing old olive trees. Grapes are as tiny as seeds with fresh tender leaves which are everywhere being made into dolmades. Olives still in flower.

Wild almonds everywhere, very bitter. Fruit forming on the pear trees. Purple and blue flower month with endemic *Ebenus cretica*, thistles, *Daucus carota*, *Arum concinatum* in the cleared spaces between vines and yellow broom.

In season: Local artichokes abundant, loquats, cherries and plums. Lettuce available but very poor quality.

June

Grapes are now pea sized. Farmers are still tying up growing grapes. Growing mountains of olive wood appear in the storeyards as the tree trimming is finished and the branches are cut up for winter fuel. The work day is separated into two periods, early morning and late afternoon. With the long days, dinners are eaten as late as 10 pm.

Acanthus and pomegranates in flower.

In season: Mountains of watermelons and honeydew melons appear. Local plums, apricots, potatoes, cucumbers, tomatoes and green peppers available, making Greek salads ubiquitous in homes and restaurants. Courgettes in such quantities in local gardens that Kostas no longer bothers to buy them for his shop. Loquats finished.

July

Farmer's work is slowing down, with shorter hours and long rest periods in the heat of the day. Wild and eating almonds are forming fruit. The meltemi (north-west wind) rips through the village bringing slightly cooler temperatures and high tempers. Cicadas begin to make a racket in all the olive trees, heralding the fierce hot season. This is also the wedding and baptism season with lots of parties. The annual village festival is celebrated on July 26 on the saint's day of Agia Paraskevi. Village life moves out to the street in the warm summer evenings and many people find it cooler to sleep on their balconies.

Hillsides turn purple with thyme and thistle flowers. The countryside is beginning to look very parched and desiccated.

In season: Courgettes, tomatoes, aubergine, melons, cucumbers, potatoes and onions plentiful. Corn, okra, pears, peaches and nectarines appear, cabbage makes a reappearance after an absence of three months.

August

This is the height of the season of celebrations, weddings and baptisms. All Athens comes to Crete for their holidays, including the Greek Prime Minister. The first two weeks are fasting days in preparation for the Feast of the Assumption of the Virgin Mary. The first of the grapes ripen and begin to appear in the cafenia and homes.

Hillsides now look very dry with only a few remaining purple thistle flowers to give colour.

In season: Pears, more melons, figs, horta from watered fields, corn, okra, early grapes.

September

Grapes in full season and raisin racks are all full of sun drying fruit. This is the season for grafting the sultana and wine varieties onto the wild Californian root stock planted in the spring. Wine making all around the village with sultana and black grapes mixed to make the village "red" wine. Wild thyme honey is made and the beehives are brought in.

The last flowers of the dry season, "turkos", in bloom. Turkos *(Urginea maritima)* are erect flowers growing from large bulbs, said to be poisonous. Michalis says that they are called turkos because the Cretans walking through the fields chop off their heads with their sticks.

In season: Almonds, pomegranates, grapes.

October

Raisins finish and grape leaves turn yellow/red. In 1995 out of date chemicals were sprayed in error on the olive groves. This resulted in a premature drop of the crop giving low quality oil and causing financial hardship. Raki making from the fermented grape pips and skins starts this month and is the excuse for late-night revelling. Quinces begin to ripen late in the month. In season: Pomegranates, almonds, chestnuts make their first appearance in the village shop, harbingers of winter and the Christmas season.

FIRST RAINS

This is a variable season but a week or two after the first good soaking rains the green reappears on the hillside, mostly from *Oxalis* and the first autumn flowers appear. Some are spring flowers making a brief mistaken appearance. *Calendula*, *Ranunculus*, autumn crocuses *(Sternbergia)*, white *heliotrope* and the first vrouves. Dandelions also appear and are known here, of course, as another variety of horta.

November

Raki making continues. November 3 is the feast of the Drunken St. George, an occasion to sample the new wine. Olive groves are prepared for picking by burning leaves and ground cover as the olives begin to ripen. Around the village winter stoves are set up and in the early morning the rooftops are swathed in the smell and smoky vision of old fashioned rural life. As the days grow shorter and colder the work day is once again consolidated into one period in the warmest part of the day.

In season: Quince, oranges and mandarins. Green vegetables appear, such as cultivated horta, including radikio and lettuce. Cabbage and cauliflower are at their height. Walnuts and chestnuts appear by the truckload, just as the winter wood stoves are set up in order to roast them.

December

The olive oil factory goes into production. Olive picking becomes a daily task on fair days. Many saint's day celebrations occur this month and pigs are fattened for the Christmas feast.

All the countryside is bright green with clover and yellow /brown with the dying leaves from the grape vines.

In season: Lettuce, cauliflower, quince, beetroot, chestnuts, large white radish, leeks.

APPENDIX TWO

SELECTED BIBLIOGRAPHY

We have read literally everything available on Crete that we have been able to find, scouring bookshops in Crete, Athens, Britain and Canada. We give below, a list of those we have found more informative on various aspects on Cretan life and natural history.

Travel Guides and General

In travelling around Crete there are two guides which we have used extensively (although they are now getting out of date) and found to be informative.

John Fisher and Geoff Garvey. 1991. Crete: the Rough Guide. Harrap Columbus, London.

Eberhard Fohrer. 1990. Crete: The Traveller's Guide. Springfield Books Ltd., Huddersfield. (Translated from German).

Miles Lambert-Gocs. 1990. The Wines of Greece. Faber and Faber, London.

Lilian B. Lawler. 1964. The Dance in Ancient Greece. Wesleyan University Press, Middletown, Connecticut.

Flora and Fauna

Bertel Bruun and Arthur Singer. 1970. The Hamlyn Guide to Birds of Britain and Europe. Hamlyn Publishing Group Ltd., London.

G. Handrinos and A. Demetropoulos. 1983. Birds of Prey of Greece. Efstathiadis Group, Athens.

Anthony Huxley and William Taylor. 1989. Flowers of Greece and the Aegean. The Hogarth Press, London.

Oleg Polunin. 1980. Flowers of Greece and the Balkans: A field Guide. Oxford University Press, Oxford.

Oleg Polunin and Anthony Huxley. 1965. Flowers of the Mediterranean. Chatto and Windus, London.

George Sfikas. 1987. Wild flowers of Crete. Efstathiadis Group, Athens.

George Sfikas. 1989. Birds and Mammals of Crete. Efstathiadis Group, Athens.

Paul Whalley. 1993. The Michael Beazley Pocket Guide to Butterflies. Michael Beazley International Ltd., London.

Village Life

Du Boulay's anthropological account is more interesting and informative, but Greger's sociological account is more directly relevant to Crete.

Juliet du Boulay. 1974. Portrait of a Greek Mountain Village. Oxford University Press, Oxford.

Scott Davies. 1997. Traditional Village Life in Crete. Toubis, Athens.

Sonia Greger. 1988. Village On The Plateau. Brewin Books, Studley, Warwickshire.

Minoans

Rodney Castleden. 1990. Minoans: Life in Bronze Age Crete. Routledge, London.

Don Everly, Helen Hughes-Brock & Nicoletta Momigliano (Eds.). 1994. Knossos, a labyrinth of history. Papers presented in honour of Sinclair Hood. The British School at Athens, Athens.

James Walter Graham. 1962. The Palaces of Crete. Princeton University Press, Princeton.

R.W. Hutchinson. 1962. Prehistoric Crete. Penguin Books Ltd., London.

Nicholas Platon. 1971. Zakros - The discovery of a lost palace of ancient Crete. Charles Scribner's Sons, New York.

R.F. Willets. 1969. Everyday Life in Ancient Crete. B.T. Batsford Ltd. London. & G.P. Putnam's Sons, New York.